Macs for Morons

Christian Boyce

Hayden
Books

Macs for Morons

Library of Congress Catalog No.: 93-80004

ISBN: 1-56830-077-8

95 94 93   4 3 2 1

Interpretation of the printing code: the rightmost double-digit number is the year of the book's printing; the rightmost single-digit number is the number of the book's printing. For example, a printing code of 93-1 shows that the first printing of the book occurred in 1993.

Publisher   David Rogelberg

Product Director   Karen Bluestein

Special Advisor   Dave Ciskowski

Development Editor   Brad Miser

Publishing Coordinator   Mat Wahlstrom

Copy Editor   M. T. Cagnina

Cover Designer   Tim Amrhein

Interior Designers   Michael Nolan, Kevin Spear

Illustrators   Kathy Hanley, Doug Bobilya

Production Coordinator   Mary Beth Wakefield

Indexers   Jeanne Clark

Production Team   Gary Adair, Ayrika Bryant, Brad Chinn,
                         Tim Cox, Meshell Dinn, Karen Dodson,
                         Mark Enochs, Diana Bigham-Griffin, Beth
                         Rago, Marc Shecter

Composed in Stone Informal and Stone Sans Serif

About the Author

Christian Boyce

Beverly Hills-based Christian Boyce is the Macintosh consultant to the stars. Formerly a Rocket Scientist, and currently a Darned Funny Guy, Christian's ability to translate techno-jargon into standard English makes *Macs for Morons* readable, informative, and downright fun. Christian has taught hundreds of non-technical people to use and enjoy their Macs, and he can do the same for you.

Official Credits

Official "Macs for Morons" back cover photographer: Bill Knapp Photography, Los Angeles, California.

Official "Macs for Morons" shareware game: Maelstrom 1.2 by Andrew Welch.

Official "Macs for Morons" shareware screen-capture utility (used to take the pictures): Flash-It! 3.0.2 by Nobu Toge.

Official "Macs for Morons" motto: "Get hot, baby."

Mr. Boyce's wardrobe by Mervyn's of Southern California.

Acknowledgments

Of all the people who encouraged me to write this book, Karen Bluestein was most instrumental. Interestingly, she was also most vocal. Karen's a one-woman band.

Laura Wirthlin helped me hatch this book during MacWorld Expo 1992 as we sat in traffic on an impossibly-over-crowded Boston freeway. She also laughed at my jokes (now there's something worth acknowledging).

Tom Beyrle kept me on the straight and narrow when it came to explaining how "simple" things work. I'd send him a draft, sure it was perfect, and Tom would prove it wasn't. Many a rewritten paragraph owes its final wording to Tom.

Becky Yang handled all administrative duties associated with getting the manuscript to the publisher's offices. Hayden's Mat Wahlstrom took it from there. Each did yeoman's work; a heartfelt "Thanks!" to both.

Friends and family contributed significantly with countless words of encouragement. I must have heard "I can't believe you're still not done!" fifty times a day, especially as my deadline approached. To be fair, forty of those times it was Karen Bluestein on the line... regardless, the message sank in, and finally I finished. Truly I'm grateful. Really.

Finally, thanks to you for buying the book. And watch for "Macs for Morons: The Movie," coming to a theater near you, depending on where you live. If by some miracle the movie's ever finished (heck, it'd be a miracle if the movie's ever *started*), the popcorn will be on me. I mean it.

Christian Boyce

September 1993

We Want to Hear from You

Dear Friend,

I want to thank you on behalf of everyone at Hayden Books for choosing "Macs for Morons" to help you learn to use and enjoy your Macintosh. Expanding your knowledge base can be challenging without the right book. We have carefully crafted this book to make learning the Macintosh as simple and entertaining as possible.

What our readers think of our books is important to our ability to better serve you in the future. If you have any comments, no matter how great or small, we'd appreciate you taking the time to send us a note. Of course, great book ideas are always welcomed.

Sincerely yours,

David Rogelberg
Publisher, Hayden Books and Adobe Press

We can be reached at the following address:

David Rogelberg, Publisher
Hayden Books
201 West 103rd Street
Indianapolis, IN 46290

(800) 428-5331 voice
(800) 448-3804 fax

Electronic mail:

America Online:	HaydenBks
AppleLink:	hayden.books
CompuServe:	76350,3014
Internet:	hayden@hayden.com

Table of Contents at a Glance

Table of Contents

You're Gonna Love It!

Remember getting your driver's license? It gave you freedom, and it expanded your world. Assuming you were able to beg, borrow, or steal a car (and it didn't much matter which), you could go anywhere–and fast. Driving a car gave you power to do things you'd previously been unable to do; you could carry a ton of groceries home in one trip, and you could (finally!) take that girl in your Spanish class to the movies.

Learning to drive a car was great. Learning to use a Mac should be similar. Notice I said "should be." I said it that way because, quite frankly, it usually ain't.

Learning to use a Mac ought to make you wax romantic. You should say, "Ah, yes, I remember learning to use a Mac. First day, I made a Valentine for that girl in my Spanish class." Instead, you say "Was I absent the day they passed out computer savvy? Everyone knows what they're talking about but me." It's a sad state of affairs, but at least there's Someone To Blame; unfortunately, it's me. Well, not just me. Me and practically everyone else who's written about computers and how to use them. Blame it on the authors. It happened like this:

First, we learned to use Macs, by hook or by crook. Then, with the learning behind us and the process forgotten, we fell for that "user-friendly" nonsense. (And why not? The Mac was user-friendly—once we knew how to use it.) Then (and this is the key step), we wrote manuals, books, or both, and we forgot to start with the basics. We forgot that the Way of the Mac was not second nature. And we forgot who we were writing for.

Sorry about that. This book will set things right.

What You'll Learn

This book will teach you to use a Mac. That means that you'll be able to sit down at your Mac, or *any* Mac, and do something useful, fun, or both at the same time. It will also teach you enough to impress members of The Great Unknowing, including your boss (unless he's read this book).

N
O
t
E
(You'll find Notes like this— indicated with the official Note symbol— sprinkled throughout the book. Read them for commentary, illumination, and the occasional bad joke.)

It's important that you understand the difference between learning to use a Mac and learning to use a particular company's computer program. It's the difference between just plain learning to drive versus learning to drive your dad's car. When you get that learner's permit, you just want to learn to drive. Same with the Mac: once you know how to use it, you'll be able to handle any computer program the world throws at you.

For my part, I assume that you're a beginner, with little computer experience. I also assume that you're less interested in *learning* to use a Mac than you are in actually getting down to *using* one. No problem. I'll keep that in mind.

What You Won't Learn

This is an introductory and *general* book. You won't find a lot of technical mumbo-jumbo, nor instructions for building your own Macintosh from chips available at Radio Shack. You won't find a complete treatment of any single subject; rather, you'll find just enough stuff on just enough subjects to be able to get things done. If you're looking for specifics, you're in the wrong place. But if you're looking for a beginner's guidebook, you've found it.

How This Book is Organized

There's more Mac stuff to know now than there used to be. Fortunately, you don't need to know everything before doing some work. That's why I've split this book into these parts:

- The Basics (chapters 1–4). Really and truly basic. Required reading. Life or death. Enough Mac stuff to get you up and running and doing work. An occasional bad joke.

- Important but Delayable (chapters 5–7). For when you're comfortable with the basics. Not life or death, but lots of good stuff. More bad jokes.

- Care and Feeding (chapters 8–9). Routine maintenance. Trouble shooting. Even more bad jokes.

- Extra Bonus (Appendices A and B). Words that let you sound like a genius. Tips that let you work like one.

In case you haven't noticed the kind where there's an awful lot of Mac stuff to know. The tricky part was figuring out how to tell you. The fact that everything's connected to everything else makes a linear "Step 1, step 2,...step six zillion and nine" kind of book impossible to write.

Therefore, I've sprinkled this book with parenthetical sidebars and comments, (things that don't quite fit in the text but are still worth your time). Look for the following symbols as you read through the book.

NOTE *Sometimes there's more to say than most people want to know. In the interest of being complete, and for those who crave knowledge, I've included muchos juicy Mac knowledge nuggets under the Notes icon.*

I hate to use techno-jargon, but everyone else does it and you might as well know what they're saying. Mac Lingos put it into English for you.

There's almost always more than one way to do something on a Mac. In most cases, there's an easy, but somewhat clumsy way and a brilliant, somewhat hidden, but clearly much better way. Genius Tips reveal the secrets.

One of my favorite parts of this book was revealing my favorite shortcuts. Take Command sidebars teach you shortcuts to make your Mac life easier.

This should be self-explanatory, but when you're paid by the word you don't mind stating the obvious. Quite simply, there are times when you ought to take extra care; Big Trouble sidebars point these out, before it's too late.

Hopefully, this layout makes more sense than the standard bore-you-with-stuff-that-doesn't-mean-anything-to-you organizational scheme. It's harder for me but easier for you.

Conventions

No, I'm not talking about, the kind where you go to some fancy hotel and goof-off for a week. I'm talking about the conventions I've used to make this book more understandable. Here they are:

- Menu names and menu selections are shown in **bold**.

- Stuff you are supposed to type is in a special `typeface that looks like this`.

- The names of specific keys that you need to use begin with a Capital letter (such as Return, Shift, and Command).

- The names of buttons that you need to use also begin with a Capital letter (for example, Save, Print, and Cancel).

Enough yakking. Let's get started.

Chapter 1
Ultra Basics

Let's take it from the top, shall we?

In this chapter, you'll learn a couple of words that'll help us understand each other. Then, you'll learn to turn your Mac on, turn your Mac off, and fool around with the mouse in between.

Meet Your Mac

They can put a man on the Moon but they can't decide what a Mac should look like. Some Macs are portable all-in-one devices. Other Macs are desktop-bound collections of individual units. Regardless, each Mac includes the following parts:

- A *keyboard*. It's like the keyboard on a typewriter, only different. Computer snobs call it an "input device." Figure 1.1 shows two common Macintosh keyboards.

- A *monitor*. This looks something like a TV, and it acts something like a TV, though its programming is usually better. *You* probably don't need a picture to recognize a monitor, but other people might. Figure 1.2 is for them. Note: monitors are often called "screens."

- A *mouse*. This is the bar-of-soap-sized plastic gizmo with a cord coming out of one end. This is also an "input device." Apple occasionally refines their mouse design; figure 1.3 shows some of them.

- A *central processing unit*, or *CPU*. The Central Processing Unit is the brains of the thing; look for a box with lots of cables attached to it. Figure 1.4 shows some popular CPUs. Note that your Mac's model name is somewhere on the CPU.

Figure 1.1
Macintosh keyboards

Figure 1.2
Some common monitors

Figure 1.3
Some common mice

Nobody says central processing unit. Instead, they say CPU. So should you, if you want to be understood. Pronounce each letter separately: "See-Pee-Yew."

Technically, the CPU is the computer chip inside the box, not the box itself. I assume you'll overlook this fine point.

Figure 1.4
Some popular CPUs

Some Macs combine the monitor and the CPU into a single unit. These are called compact, or *Classic*, Macs (figure 1.5).

Other Macs combine the monitor, the CPU, the keyboard, and the mouse (in the form of a trackball) into a single unit. These Macs are called *PowerBooks* (figure 1.6). They are also called *laptop computers*.

Figure 1.5
Compact Mac

For our purposes, it doesn't matter what kind of Mac you've got or what it looks like. All are welcome here. Amazingly, it doesn't matter which Mac you learn on—everything you learn can be applied to other Macs.

Figure 1.6
A PowerBook

Turning On Your Mac

Oh, sure, I could make some cheap joke about whispering sweet nothings, but the *Macs for Morons* reader is far too classy for that. You want answers! You want results! You want The Keys to the Macintosh Universe!

On the other hand, maybe you don't. Maybe you'd rather have the joke. Tough beans, Bucko. The jokes are in chapter 2.

Turning on your Mac is either "easy" or "super easy." We'll deal with "super easy" first; if that doesn't work for you, try "easy."

(PowerBook users should skip ahead to "Turning on Your PowerBook" later in this chapter. Nothing wrong with reading everything, however, just for fun.)

Super-easy method for turning on your Mac:

Press the Startup key on your keyboard. The Startup key is the one with the small triangle on it. It's either near the top edge or in the upper right-hand corner of the keyboard. Figure 1.7 shows what you're looking for.

note
There's a chance that your Mac has an external hard disk, and even though you aren't supposed to know what that does yet, you've got to have it switched on before turning on your Mac. If you see a phone-book sized box connected to your Mac with a thick cable, you've got an external hard disk; look on the box for a power switch and switch the thing on. While you're at it, switch on everything else that's connected to your Mac too.

(PowerBook keyboards don't have Startup keys. I told you guys, skip ahead to the PowerBook section!)

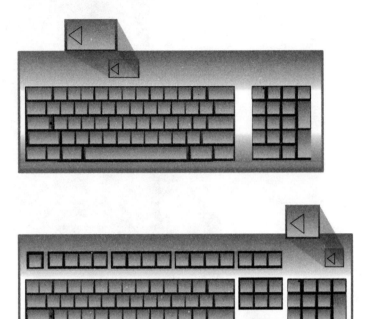

Figure 1.7
Keyboard Startup key

note The Desktop is created by a computer program called the Finder. You'll learn all about the Finder in Chapter 7, but you'll be ahead of the game if you understand that the Finder is responsible for making your Mac look like a Mac. You'll be further ahead if you understand that the Finder runs automatically every time you

With luck, something happened; with more luck, "something" was a 'bing' noise and perhaps a soft whirring sound. If you heard a bing, look at the monitor. See anything besides pure blackness? Perhaps a little box with "Welcome to Macintosh" in it?

If you do, you're done. You've turned on your Mac! Way to go. If you heard the 'bing' but didn't get a picture on the monitor, look for a power button on the monitor itself. Press the button and hope for the best. Either way, eventually you should see what's pictured in figure 1.8, called—officially—*The Macintosh Desktop*. You'll learn all about the Desktop in chapter 2. For now, just remember the name.

start your Mac, and you'll be further ahead than that if you under-stand that the Finder is always running, as long as your Mac is turned on.

Think of the Desktop as your Mac's home base, and think of the Finder as the Desktop's creator. It's really as simple as that.

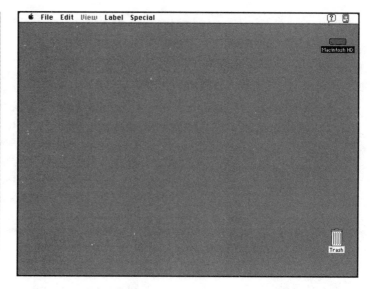

Figure 1.8
The Macintosh Desktop

Heard a bing, switched on the monitor, and still no picture? Look for brightness and contrast controls (either dials or buttons on the monitor's case, or maybe on the Mac itself). Fiddle with them until a picture appears.

If you didn't hear a bing it's probably not your fault. Most likely, your Mac's Startup key simply doesn't work. This doesn't signal a defective Mac; instead, it signals a defective *design*, one in which Apple saves twelve cents per Mac by omitting the Startup key electronics. Sorry to say, you will have to turn on your Mac the old-fashioned way.

Easy method for turning on your Mac (it ain't "super easy" but it's still not hard. At most, two steps):

1. Locate and flip the CPU's power switch. (Some Macs have a "rocker" switch in the back; others have a push-button in the front.)

   You ought to hear a bing.

2. If necessary, locate and flip the monitor's power switch. This switch is usually a push-button or rocker switch on the front or back of the monitor's case. That's not so hard.

Now it's your turn; those of you who don't have a PowerBook may skip the next section.

note *You say you've followed my directions to the letter, but the machine won't respond? Have no fear, I won't leave you high and dry, look in Chapter 9 for troubleshooting tips.*

note *Some PowerBooks, called Duos, don't have a round "on" button behind a door. Instead, they have an oblong "on" button, located above the top row of keys on the keyboard.*

If you try to turn on a PowerBook that is already on, you will lose whatever work you haven't saved. For goodness sake, try waking it up first.

Turning On Your PowerBook

The typical Macintosh is either on or off. PowerBooks are different: they can be on, off, or somewhere in between. The in-between state, called "sleep," is a sort of hibernation mode designed to save your PowerBook's batteries when you leave the thing on. Sleeping dims the screen until it's black and cuts power to the rest of the computer almost entirely—but it doesn't turn the machine off. Not quite, anyway.

Waking a sleeping PowerBook is easier than 'super-easy:' press any key, any key at all. Your PowerBook's screen will light up and you'll hear a soft 'pop' from the speaker. That's normal, by the way. You'll then hear a whirring sound, and literally seconds later, your PowerBook will be ready for action.

A shut-off PowerBook looks exactly like a sleeping one. Pressing a key on the keyboard won't do a thing for a shut-off PowerBook, but you should always assume a black-screened PowerBook is sleeping, not off. You'll understand why as soon as you know how to turn on a shut-off PowerBook (which, coincidentally, is the subject of the very next paragraph; hang in there).

Turning a shut-off PowerBook on isn't easier than 'super-easy,' but it's easily "easy." Simply open the wide door on the back edge of the PowerBook and press the only push button you find (it's round). You'll hear a 'bong' and a whir, and shortly you'll see a "Welcome to Macintosh" message on the screen.

It's important to realize that pressing the "on" switch, whether on a PowerBook, a Duo, or any other Mac, completely restarts the machine. If you happen to be working on something when you press the switch, you'll probably lose some work. Since PowerBooks go to sleep by themselves, the odds are good that you will have a file open when the machine dozes off. Thus, pressing the "on" switch is a no-no, because that technique will cause you to lose important work. Pressing a key on the keyboard will simply bring the machine back to life, and your work will be just as you left it. All of which may be summarized in a single rule:

Always assume a black-screened PowerBook is sleeping, not turned off.

Your first move with a black-screened PowerBook, then, should be a press of a key on the keyboard. If the PowerBook doesn't respond, go for the "on" button.

Regardless of how you turned on your Mac, your screen should look like figure 1.8. You're ready to learn how to use the mouse.

How to Use a Mouse

n O t E *Mice don't have power switches. When the CPU's on, the mouse is on.*

If you've gotten this far, learning to use a mouse will be easy. First, pick the thing up and turn it over. See the little ball? Good. That ball is the key to everything. You'll see why in a minute.

Place the mouse right side up, with the cord facing away from you, on a flat surface. Most people use a desk, but you're welcome to use a pancake, the top of your head, an anvil, whatever. Slide the mouse around while watching the monitor. Notice anything? You should.

n O t E *PowerBooks don't have mice. Instead they have trackballs. When I say "roll the mouse around," PowerBook users have to translate that to "roll the trackball around."*

PowerBook trackballs have two buttons (a mouse has only one) but both do exactly the same thing. So, when I say, "Click the mouse button" PowerBook users have to translate that to "Click either of the trackball buttons." I tell you, it's a hard life.

You should see a little arrow (figure 1.9) that moves when you move the mouse. Slide the mouse to the left and the arrow moves left. Slide the mouse to the right and the arrow moves right. Figure 1.10 shows how it works: mouse left, arrow left; mouse right, arrow right. Cha-cha-cha. This isn't something that comes naturally, but stick with it. Everyone is awkward at first.

Figure 1.9
The arrow cursor

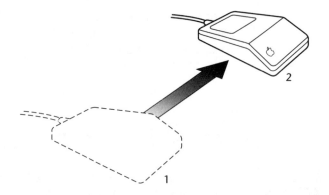

That little arrow on the screen is called the "pointer." It's also called the "arrow cursor."

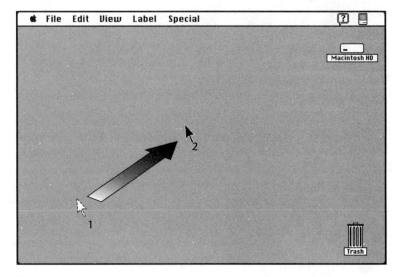

Figure 1.10
Doing the mouse cha-cha-cha

Pick the mouse up and wave it around. Notice any action on the screen? You *shouldn't*. If that little mouse-ball isn't rolling, the pointer won't move. This factoid (factoid, *n*: small fact) means that you can pick the mouse up and set it down some-where else when you run out of room on your desk. Try this "lint brush technique" (sliding the mouse on your desk from point A to point B, then *lifting* the mouse, setting it down at point A again, and sliding it back toward B again), beautifully illustrated, á la Arthur Murray, in figure 1.11. A-one, and a-two, and a-three. It works.

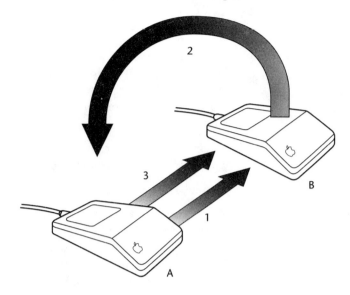

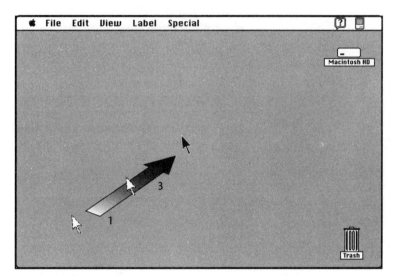

Figure 1.11
My, you glide so gracefully across the screen

Keep moving the mouse around until you feel at least a little less clumsy than before. Break for coffee (the official hot beverage of the *Macs for Morons* creative team), orange juice, jet fuel, or whatever it is you drink. Then come back ready to work. You're one-third of the way to Total Mouse Mastery, which is fairly impressive for someone so young, but there are still two parts to go.

Moving the mouse around is fine, but what's the point? All you've done is slide an arrow around on the screen. Big deal.

Actually, it *is* a big deal. Here's why.

Everything you do on a Mac, and I mean everything, happens in this order: first you select something, then you do something to it. The sequence is critical. Select, then do. Subject, then verb. Thing, then action. Ice cream, then eat. Résumé, then print. Lawyer, then kick. Mac book, then read.

You'll learn several ways to select things on a Macintosh, but none is more basic than the aptly-named *click*. Clicking is easy: just press and release the button on the mouse.

The trick, as you've probably surmised, is to click in the right place. And how do you get to the right place? By moving the pointer (by moving the mouse). Let's give it a try:

1. Move the mouse until the tip of the pointer touches the trash can at the bottom right hand corner of the screen (figure 1.12).

Trash

Figure 1.12
Pointer touching the trash can

2. Press and release the mouse button.

   The trash can should turn dark, as in figure 1.13.

Trash

Figure 1.13
Dark trash can

The button on the mouse is known as the "mouse button." What will they think of next?

The trash can is called—drum roll, please—"the Trash." You'll learn to use it later. For now, it's enough to know its name.

GENIUS TIP

It's the tip of the arrow that counts. Be sure the tip is touching the Trash when you click.

Pointing to something, then clicking on it, is called "selecting." When an object is selected, it turns dark. You'll select things every time you use a Mac.

You know how to move the arrow cursor around (point), and you know how to select something (click). Two down, one to go: time to learn how to *drag*.

Suppose you wanted to drag a piece of paper across your real desk. You'd move your hand over the paper, touch the paper with a finger, slide your finger (and the paper underneath) to the desired location, then lift your finger and go your merry way. The paper would stay where you left it.

Dragging things on the Mac is exactly the same. We'll practice by dragging the Trash around.

1. Click on the Trash, except this time keep holding the mouse button down.

2. Keep the button down while sliding the mouse away from you a couple of inches.

   Notice that an outline of the Trash is attached to the pointer. You should see something like figure 1.14.

Figure 1.14
Dragging the Trash

3. Let go.

   The Trash jumps to where you let go of the mouse button. Isn't this easy?

That's it: pointing, clicking, and dragging. Nothing to it. If you want some practice, try dragging the Trash back to where you found it. Remember: use the tip of the arrow, click just once (and hold it down), and let go when you're through. It's easy.

Had enough? Let's turn the thing off.

Turning Off Your Mac

There's one right way and about a million wrong ways to turn off your Mac, even if it's a PowerBook. Here are several wrong ways:

- Flip the power switch.

- Pull the plug.

- Zap it with a cattle prod.

- Douse it with water until it's safely out.

- Blot (don't rub) until it disappears.

The right way is called "Choosing **Shut Down** from the **Special** menu." Here's how it's done.

1. Move the pointer to the top of the screen until the pointer points to **Special**.

2. Click on the word **Special** and hold the mouse button down.

   A *menu* drops down (figure 1.15).

Figure 1.15
The **Special** menu

Menus have names; they're named after the words at their tops. Thus, the menu that dropped down when you clicked on the word Special is called the "Special menu."

3. Keeping the mouse button down, slide the pointer down the menu until **Shut Down** is selected (figure 1.16). You know **Shut Down** is selected when it's inside the dark box.

4. Let go of the mouse button.

Figure 1.16
Choosing **Shut Down** from the **Special** menu

n Shutting down is like
o parking your car
t before turning it off.
E Sure, you could simply
flip the power switch,
but that's like stopping
your car by smashing
into a tree. It works, but
it can lead to damage.

If everything goes black, far out: you're done.

If not, you'll see a message on the screen telling you it's safe to switch the power off. Just do it and be done. That's it!

Now, for those of you who have PowerBooks, go to the next section. For the rest, you may skip ahead one section if you like.

Special Bonus PowerBook Discussion

I mentioned that PowerBooks go to sleep automatically, and that's true. But you can put a PowerBook to sleep yourself if you want to, and it isn't hard: just choose **Sleep** from the **Special** menu instead of choosing **Shut Down**. This saves a little bit of battery power, but not much, since the typical PowerBook will go to sleep by itself in five minutes anyhow.

The big question in a PowerBook owner's mind should be, "Why choose **Sleep** instead of **Shut Down**? What's the difference?" Good question. The answer: PowerBooks wake up from sleep much, much more quickly than they start up from being completely shut down. Thus, if you're an impatient sort, put the thing to sleep so you can bring it back quickly. If you're not going to use your PowerBook for a couple of hours, shut it down.

Starting Over

Believe it or not, your expensive computer isn't perfect. It will, at times, completely freeze up. Nothing will happen when you move the mouse, and you won't be able to choose **Shut Down** (or anything else) from the menus. In this situation there's nothing to do but give up and start over.

Restarting gives your Mac a fresh start, clears its mind, and basically makes a lot of problems go away. You can choose **Restart** from the **Special** menu anytime you want to, assuming you can move the pointer, but that's not what this section's about. This section's about what to do when you CAN'T move the pointer.

The Good Way to Restart

Look for a button with a triangle on it (different than the Startup key) and press it. You'll find this button on the back of some Macs, on the front of others, and nowhere on still others. Pressing this button, called the "restart" switch, will momentarily turn your Mac off. After a moment, your Mac will start up normally.

If you can't even find this button, try combinations of the Control, Option, Command (the one with the apple on it), and Startup keys (for example, hold down the Control and Option keys and then hit the Startup key). If you stumble across the right combination, excellent. Write it down for future reference.

If you can't find the good way to restart, you'll have to go to the next section.

The Not-So-Good Way to Restart

There's not much difference between pressing the restart button and switching the Mac off and then on again. The restart button is more gentle, though, so you should use it (or a Startup key combination) if you can. Otherwise, turning your Mac off and then on again will restart it.

Well, now. You know what the parts of your Mac are called. You know how to turn your Mac on; you know how to use the mouse; you know how to turn your Mac off, and you know how

note *If you can't find the good way to restart, use the not-so-good way for now. When you get a minute, you should look for the good way in your owner's manual and/or call Apple. You really should know the good way to restart. I guarantee you'll need it.*

to restart it in an emergency. That's a nice day's work, so let's take five. But first, take this test:

1. Can you identify the keyboard, the mouse, the monitor, and the CPU?

2. Can you tell what kind of Mac you have?

3. Can you turn your Mac on?

4. Can you point, click, and drag?

5. Can you turn your Mac off *the right way*?

6. Can you loan me twenty bucks until Friday?

Chapter 2
Regular Basics

Now that you know how to
turn your Mac on and off,
you're ready to dive into things
and get going. Sorry to say that
there's still a lot of background
material to cover, but it can't be
helped. Learn it now, and you'll be set for
life. Or at least for the rest of this book.

This chapter introduces some important concepts that simply
must be mastered. Don't skip them. If you're feeling smart, try
the quiz at the end of the chapter. If you know all the answers,
fine—move ahead if you must. But realize that this chapter
contains all the best jokes and stories.

**Programmers are
sometimes termed
"wire heads." They
don't seem to mind.**

Use what you learned in chapter 1 and start up your Mac. You
should see something that looks like figure 2.1 on your screen.
You've seen this before; it's the Macintosh Desktop. We're going
to poke around the desktop in a minute. First, a little history.
It'll help you understand why things are the way they are.

It wasn't very long ago that personal computers looked a lot
like big computers, only smaller. Programmers and other
people familiar with big computers liked these little computers,
but no one else did.

Normal people couldn't stand the early personal computers.
Who wanted to type "c:dir" (in orange letters on a black screen)
to look inside a hard disk? The whole business was infuriatingly
cumbersome and totally nonintuitive. C:dir? Come on. A cat on
drugs could come up with something better than that.

The Macintosh development team realized that making a
computer smaller didn't make it personal. They also realized
that most of us are happier when others do things our way. So,
rather than teach us "c:dir" and a bunch of other nonsense, the
people who set up the Macintosh tried to make it like Real Life.
They gave us a *desktop* as our home-base control center, and
that made some sense. They represented the documents we
created with *pictures* that *looked* like documents (sort of), and
that made sense, too. Then they gave us *folders* to store our

documents in, and that made even more sense. Finally, they gave us a trash can for the stuff we wanted to throw away. Figure 2.2 shows some pictures representing documents, folders, and the trash.

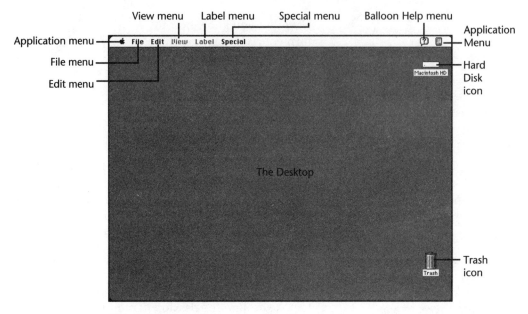

Figure 2.1
The Macintosh Desktop

Figure 2.2
Documents, folders, and the trash

Similarities between the Macintosh Desktop and your real desktop abound. For example:

- Both desktops can be cluttered with documents and folders.

- Both desktops can be standard government-issue or wildly customized.

Take another look at figure 2.2. Those little pictures of documents, folders, and the trash are called "icons." Icons are always about as big as postage stamps, except when they are the so-called small icons, which are about one-quarter as big. Macs are loaded with icons, so you may as well get used to them.

The key, of course, is recognizing that different icons represent different things. You'll learn to identify icons on sight with a bit of experience.

n Macintosh Basics is a
o program that Apple
t developed which
E teaches the basics
(hence the name) of
using the Macintosh. It is
an excellent piece of
work. I strongly recom-
mend that you go
through it at least once.

If it is not already
installed on your hard

continues

• Both desktops have a trash can on them. (Okay, that's a bit of a reach, but it's certainly possible. My real desktop *looks* like a trash can fell on it; perhaps that's close enough.)

Dissimilarities abound as well, which is really a shame, but someone has to break it to you:

• The Macintosh Desktop can clean itself up.

• The Macintosh Desktop cannot be used as an earthquake shelter.

• The Macintosh Desktop is vertical, so coffee cups slide right off.

Sorry about the dissimilarities, but that's the way it goes. Working with a Macintosh is an exercise in rules with exceptions; generally speaking, I'll tell you the rules, then I'll point out the exceptions.

You can learn all about documents, folders, and the trash by taking the guided tour called "Macintosh Basics." This tour is installed on every new Mac; in a few more pages you'll know enough to get into the tour and take it for yourself. I'd recommend taking the tour until you're sure you know what you're doing. Meanwhile, we'll work through the good stuff here, starting with a just-enough-but-not-too-much look at icons.

About Icons

Icons are pictures that represent things. It's really as simple as that. As usual, exceptions exist, but icons generally fall into one of these groups:

• Application icons (you'll learn about applications soon enough)

• Document icons (you've already seen these)

• Folder icons (you've already seen these, too)

It's unfortunate but true that the Macintosh gang, striving to avoid mass computer-phobia, made up new words for everything when they introduced the Mac. Some of the words made sense. Others are out-and-out losers. We'll start with a loser: "applications."

continued

disk, look through the floppy disks that came with your machine; it might be on one of those. Or check the Apple CD-ROM disk, if one came with your machine. Do what it takes to find that program. It is worth your time.

n *In the beginning,*
o *Apple's people-minded*
t *Steven Jobs (Father of*
E *the Macintosh) set an upper limit on the price of applications. The limit was $100. In case you haven't noticed, Jobs is long gone, Joe Montana plays football in Kansas City, and the price of an application has gone through the roof. Try $895 for a copy of PageMaker. I should have been a programmer. Or married one. Or something.*

Application Icons

Applications used to be something you filled out when you wanted something important, like a credit card, admission to college, or a date with that girl in my high school Spanish class. The Macintosh folks swiped a perfectly good word and confused the heck out of everyone by telling us that an *application* was something that helped us do work on a Macintosh. I think *computer program* (which is the phrase the Mac team was tip-toeing around) would have been fine. It happens that the words *application* and *program* are used virtually interchangeably in these hi-tech 90s, so it looks like we got confused for nothing.

Figure 2.3 shows the icons for some popular applications. That's a pretty expensive collection of icons (total retail price: almost $1,300).

Word 5.1a   Canvas™ 3.0.6   Microsoft Excel

Figure 2.3
Application icons

The icons in figure 2.3 represent different *kinds* of applications. Microsoft Word is a *word processor*. Microsoft Excel is a *spread-sheet program*. Canvas is a *drawing program*. (See? I can't even describe three applications without using the word "program" twice.)

You'll learn to use word processors and spreadsheet programs in the next couple of chapters. We'll briefly cover drawing programs in chapter 5. For now, here's a ten-cent definition of each:

- Word processors are for writing.
- Spreadsheet programs are for juggling numbers.
- Drawing programs are for drawing (that was a surprise, eh?).

Document Icons

Documents are the things you create with word processors, spreadsheet programs, and drawing programs. The term "document" makes sense; let's give the Mac team a big round

note

You've probably noticed that the icons shown in this chapter have names underneath them. All icons do. An icon's name can be as long as you like, so long as you don't want it to be more than 31 characters, and it can use any characters you like, so long as you don't want to use the colon. Other than that, there are no restrictions at all, except that you can't give two items the same name. Unless they're in different folders, but you don't know about folders yet. You will, shortly.

of applause. Document icons almost always look something like the applications used to create them; note how they reflect their lineage while still clearly being documents (figure 2.4).

A Word document   A Canvas document   An Excel document

Word 5.1a   Canvas™ 3.0.6   Microsoft Excel

Figure 2.4
Icons for documents and their parent applications

Document icons represent letters to Mom, birthday cards, sales records, you name it. Think of documents this way: If you can print it, it's a document. (As usual, there are exceptions to this rule, but they're so unnatural and obscure that I'll make an exception to my own rule and not tell you what the exceptions are.) Think of documents as the things you make, and applications as the tools you use to make them, and you'll be on the right track.

Folder Icons

Folder icons are easy to spot. They look like miniature manila folders and, mostly, they all look the same. There are three big exceptions (exceptions? what a surprise!) and a bunch of smaller ones that we'll run into shortly. For now, I'll show you the big ones.

Don't call folders "files." That'll confuse everyone you talk to. Files is an okay term for documents, and it's an okay name for everything on your hard disk, but it's a lousy synonym for folders. You have to know the language so you can ask for what you want, so get this one straight.

Folders are for holding things. They can hold applications, documents, other folders, you name it. That's all they're meant to do, and they do a good job of it. (You'll practice making folders, renaming them, and moving icons into and out of them soon.) Two of the three big exceptions are your Macintosh's System Folder (which runs your Mac and is Very Important) and your Macintosh's hard disk (which holds everything you have). Figure 2.5 shows the icons for a standard folder, the System Folder, and a typical hard disk.

note You can have as many folders as you want; your Mac can handle 'em all.

Standard folder

System Folder

Macintosh HD

Figure 2.5
Standard folder, System Folder, and hard disk icon

The Trash Icon

Figure 2.6 shows the icons for the full and empty Trash, which you met in chapter 1. This is Big Exceptional Folder number 3—just an ordinary folder with some extraordinary properties. For one thing, the Trash gets two icons (one for when it's empty, and one for when it's not), neither of which look anything like a manila folder. For another, the Trash is the only folder designed to hold things *temporarily*. Finally, though you can make and name as many standard folders as you wish, you cannot make a second Trash, and you cannot rename the one you've got.

Trash

Trash

Figure 2.6
Full and empty Trash icons

Big tROuBLe

Every Mac should have one (and only one) System Folder. If your Mac's got two, or more, get some help right away. One of those System Folders has to go, and you want to toss the right one (or is it the wrong one?). You'll learn more about the System Folder in chapter 7. For now, keep your mitts off of it.

mAc LiNGO

For some reason, System Folder is always capitalized as shown. System folder is wrong, and so is system folder. I can't tell you why this is, but this is the way it is.

Let's practice a bit to be sure we know what we're doing. We'll make a new folder, name it, then (after quickly becoming bored with it) drag it to the Trash. Here goes:

1. Restart your Mac by choosing **Restart** from the **Special** menu. Immediately hold a Shift key down and keep it down until your Mac's completely started up.

   You'll see the message "Extensions Off" along the way. Your Mac's screen should look a lot like figure 2.7.

2. Choose **New Folder** from the **File** menu. Figure 2.8 shows what you're looking for.

   Your Mac's screen should now look like figure 2.9. Pretty cool, eh? You actually did something!

n *I had you restart with*
o *the Shift key because it*
t *gives your Mac a gen-*
E *eric look. A generic*
Mac is one I can pre-
dict—without the Shift
key, your screen might
look very different than
the illustrations lovingly
prepared, at no small
expense of time nor
effort, by your humble
author. If you don't see
the "Extensions Off"
message, try it again,
but this time be quicker
with the Shift key. It'll
help me help you.

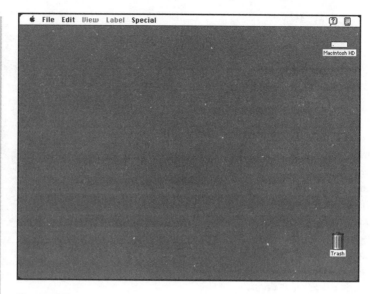

Figure 2.7
After the Shift key; a very neat desktop

File	
New Folder	⌘N
Open	⌘O
Print	⌘P
Close Window	⌘W
Get Info	⌘I
Sharing...	
Duplicate	⌘D
Make Alias	
Put Away	⌘Y
Find...	⌘F
Find Again	⌘G
Page Setup...	
Print Desktop...	

Figure 2.8
New Folder in the **File** menu

Notice that your new folder's name is "untitled folder." You can name it anything you want (remembering that 31 characters is all you get and that colons are prohibited). Let's name ours, "Coffee Grounds." Notice also that the folder's name is bordered (figure 2.10). This means it's ready for you to type something over it. Thus, all you do is type `Coffee Grounds`.

Nobody knows this, but it works: If you click on an icon (the picture, not the name), then press either the Enter or Return key, you'll get the border around the icon's name immediately. Judicious use of this tip will save you nearly fifteen seconds per year. It doesn't sound like much, but it adds up.

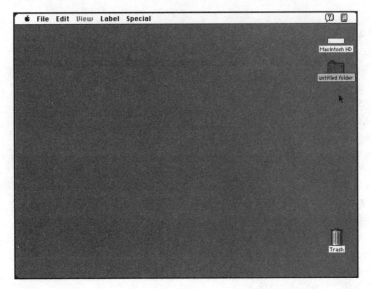

Figure 2.9
Desktop with a new, untitled folder

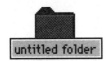

Figure 2.10
Folder with name bordered

Your new folder is now called "Coffee Grounds." If you made a mistake, get that border around the name again, by either using the genius tip or by clicking on the name and waiting a moment, and give it another go.

You wouldn't ordinarily make and name a folder just to throw it away. Here, however, you will, because it gives us something safe to toss.

Let's drag the Coffee Grounds folder to the Trash.

1. Drag the Coffee Grounds folder toward the Trash icon until the Trash icon turns black (remember, you learned to *drag* in chapter 1). Note that on a color monitor, it actually turns a dark gray, but it's the same thing.

2. Let go of the mouse button.

   The Trash becomes fat, unless it was already fat; in that case, the Trash *stays* fat.

The act of turning black is called "highlighting", as in "until the Trash icon is highlighted."

n
O *Technically, the Trash*
t *is never "full" because*
E *it's really a bottomless*
pit. An empty Trash is
easy to spot; so is a
Trash with something in
it, but you can't tell how
much is in there unless
you open the Trash and
look. One big item, ten
small items, you'll never
tell by looking at the
Trash's icon. Maybe
someday they'll make a
Trash that gets fatter
and fatter as you throw
more things into it. Or
one that oozes over the
side when it's really
loaded up.

We are about to empty the
Trash. Everything in it will
be gone forever after we
do. Be absolutely sure that
this will not ruin your day.
Read on to learn how to
get things out of the Trash.

Suppose you want to get the Coffee Grounds (or anything else) out of the Trash. Nothing to it: just open the Trash, take your Coffee Grounds out, and then close the Trash again (just like Real Life). You can do this because the Trash doesn't empty itself (also just like Real Life). Here's how:

1. Click once on the Trash icon to select it.

   The Trash icon should be black when you're done.

2. Choose **Open** from the **File** menu (figure 2.11).

File	
New Folder	⌘N
Open	⌘O
Print	⌘P
Close Window	⌘W
Get Info	⌘I
Sharing...	
Duplicate	⌘D
Make Alias	
Put Away	⌘Y
Find...	⌘F
Find Again	⌘G
Page Setup...	
Print Desktop...	

Figure 2.11
Choosing Open from the File menu

The Trash opens up and you see your folder called "Coffee Grounds." Figure 2.12 shows how it looks if you've got just the one item in the Trash.

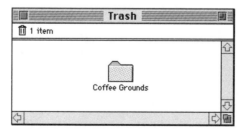

Figure 2.12
Coffee Grounds in the Trash

n o t E *Unlike Real Life, the Macintosh Trash doesn't compost your discards into a pile of goo. Theoretically, you can leave things in the Trash for years and they'll come out as fresh as they went in. I wouldn't recommend this, though; it only takes a second to empty the Trash, and one day you or someone else is going to do it without thinking and you'll become very unhappy. If you routinely leave stuff in there that you want, you're bound to lose it sooner or later.*

I know I haven't told you what a window is. I will in a minute.

3. Click on the Coffee Grounds folder, hold the mouse button down, and drag the folder completely out of the Trash window. Figure 2.13 shows the Coffee Grounds folder completely out of the Trash window, ready to be released.

Figure 2.13
Coffee Grounds completely out of the Trash window

4. Let go of the mouse button.

5. Click on the square box at the top left-hand corner of the Trash's window. Figure 2.14 shows you where to click. Remember that it's the tip of the pointer that counts.

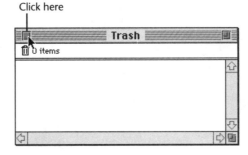

Figure 2.14
Where to click to close the window

You now know how to retrieve things from the Trash. No one will know that your Coffee Grounds were ever in the Trash at all (there's no yuckiness or damage or any other kind of a trail). Things that come out of the Trash can be used without any concern—they're as good as new.

Finally, let's put something into the Trash and empty the rascal. Three easy steps:

1. Drag the Coffee Grounds folder to the Trash. Be sure the Trash highlights before you let go of the mouse button.

   At this point, the Trash should be fat.

If there's anything else in the Trash that you think you want to save, drag it out of the Trash now. We are going to empty the trash. And you can say bye-bye to anything in there when we do.

2. Choose **Empty Trash...** from the **Special** menu (figure 2.15).

Figure 2.15
Choosing **Empty Trash...** from the **Special** menu

You'll get a box like figure 2.16 warning you that there's something in the Trash. This is the only warning you'll get, so think it over. If you're sure the stuff can go, move on to Step 3. If you want it back, no problem. Right?

Figure 2.16
Are you sure you want to empty the Trash?

That box with the message in it is an example of a "dialog box." You'll see lots of these.

3. Click once on the button labeled "OK".

The Trash becomes thin again.

If the Trash happens to hold a *locked item*, you'll get a message like figure 2.17.

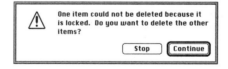

Figure 2.17
Locked items dialog box

The button labeled "OK" is called the "OK button." Isn't that special?

If an item is locked, it's probably because someone thought it was important. You should look in the Trash and see what's going on. If the file's truly garbage, you can delete it using the powerful Option key technique: hold the Option key down and choose **Empty Trash** from the **Special** menu.

note

Sharp-eyed readers will notice that the ellipsis after the word "Trash" disappears when the Option key is down. This means you don't get any warnings—just pure, garbage-destroying action.

Disk Icons

You know what a hard disk icon looks like (take a look at figure 2.5 again, or the top right area of your Mac's monitor). A second kind of disk icon, the so-called floppy disk icon, is shown in figure 2.18.

Call me Mr. Floppy

Figure 2.18
Floppy disk icon

note

Most Macs accept floppy disks through a slot in the front of the CPU, but PowerBooks take them in on the right hand side. Duos, those special PowerBooks that seem to be the exceptions to every rule, don't have floppy drives at all. If you've got a Duo, you can't use a floppy disk unless you've connected your Duo to a special Duo Dock. If you're able to do that, you'll be able to figure out where the floppy disk goes.

You've got to like this icon—it looks almost exactly like the real thing. Contrast this with the hard disk icon, which looks like a phone book. Figure *that* one out.

While you're figuring out why hard disk icons look like phone books, you might take a moment to ponder the "floppy" in floppy disk. They don't seem so floppy to me. As usual, there are good explanations for both; as usual, the explanation is good for nothing more than impressing the local Mac know-it-all. Here I go, anyway.

Hard disk icons look like phone books because the first Macintosh hard disks actually did look like phone books. These were external devices that fit beneath the Macs of the day, which took—as it happens—about as much desk space as a phone book. Today, of course, the icon makes no sense at all, especially since hard disks are inside our Macs and most of us have no idea what they look like.

Floppy disks are called "floppy" because they were based on the floppy disks used in other computers. Those disks really were floppy, especially compared to hard disks, which were metal and stiff as boards. The Mac's "floppy" disks are encased in a hard plastic shell, making them much more durable (and much less floppy) than their no-shell ancestors. Too bad for us that the "floppy" name stuck.

note
If you don't get the message of figure 2.19, the disk has already been initialized and you should see a nice floppy disk icon appear on your Desktop.

New floppy disks need to be readied for use in a Mac. The process is called *initializing*. You have to do this because (just to make life more complicated) IBM PCs now use the same "floppy" disks that Macs do, but in a different way. If you have a new floppy disk, stuff it into the Mac—metal end first, with the round silver thing toward the ground. You'll get a message like figure 2.19.

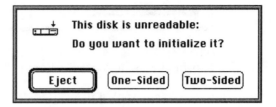

Figure 2.19
Initialize this disk?

Go ahead and initialize the disk. Click on the button labeled "Two-Sided," or on the button labeled "Initialize," if that shows up instead. If you don't have a new disk to initialize, insert a disk that's already initialized (but don't initialize it again). We'll need it for some practice.

First, let's name our floppy disk:

1. Click on the floppy disk's icon.

2. Press Enter (or Return).

    This is the shortcut we learned a while back.

3. Type Foreign Lands.

You've just renamed the disk. (Remember how you did this, so that you can change it back if you want.)

note
Clicking on the desktop tells the Mac to make the folder on the desktop and not on the floppy or the hard disk. This way, it's easy for us to find the folder and use it in this example.

Now let's make a new folder and copy it to the floppy disk.

1. Click anywhere on the desktop except on an icon.

2. Choose **New Folder** from the **File** menu (you've done this before).

3. Name the new folder in the usual way. Let's call it Texas.

4. Click on the Texas folder and drag it to the floppy disk.

You should get a message box like figure 2.20, telling you that the folder is being copied to the floppy disk. If you're using a fast Mac, look quickly.

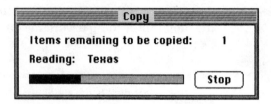

Figure 2.20
Copying the folder onto the floppy disk

Just like that, the folder is copied to the floppy disk. Don't believe me? Take a look for yourself:

1. Click on the floppy disk icon.

2. Choose **Open** from the **File** menu (figure 2.21).

Figure 2.21
Choosing Open from the File menu

And there's your Texas folder, right where it should be (on a floppy disk called "Foreign Lands"). Figure 2.22 shows how it looks if you started with a new disk.

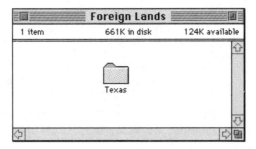

Figure 2.22
Texas folder on Foreign Lands disk

Notice that there's a Texas folder on the desktop, right where
you created it. You didn't *move* the Texas folder—you *copied* it.
This is very important. You'll see why in a minute.

You opened up your floppy disk a minute ago. Click on the
window called Foreign Lands (it's the thing that appeared when
you opened the floppy). Now:

1. Choose **New Folder** from the **File** menu.

   The new, untitled folder appears *in the Foreign Lands
   window*.

2. Name the new folder Austin. Figure 2.23 shows how it
   looks.

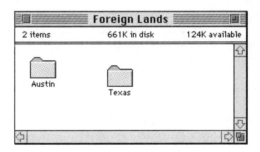

Figure 2.23
Austin and Texas folders in Foreign Lands window

3. Drag the Austin folder to the Texas folder (until the Texas
   folder turns black).

Notice that you *don't* get the dialog box of figure 2.20. Why?
Because you aren't copying. Instead, you're *moving*. This is
worth writing down (I'll do it):

GENIUS TIP

*Notice anything here? New
folders show up where you
last clicked. Click on the
Desktop and the next new
folder shows up on the
Desktop. Click on the
Foreign Lands window and
the next new folder shows
up in the Foreign Lands
window. Remember this the
next time you want to
make a folder.*

When you drag something from one place on a disk to another place on the *same* disk you're *moving* it. When you drag something from one disk to another disk you're *copying* it. Thus, you can rearrange your hard disk (move stuff around) by making new folders and dragging things into them, and you can make *copies* of things on your hard disk by dragging them onto floppy disks. It's pretty straightforward: *same disk = moving, different disks = copying.*

One last thing you need to know about floppy disks: how to get them out of your Mac. It's easy, but I'm warning you, it's going to seem weird. Trust me this time.

1. Click on the floppy disk icon.

2. Drag it to the Trash (no kidding) and let go.

Believe it or not, this is the best way to eject a disk. I agree that it's the least intuitive procedure we've covered so far. And no, we didn't erase the disk (put it back in and look at it, if you don't believe me).

Enough about icons. It's time to learn about menus. Before we do, let's break for coffee.

About Menus

You've already seen the **File** and **Special** menus; this section will briefly introduce you to the others (and tell you a little bit more about **File** and **Special** as well).

Let's take it from the left to the right, reading across the top of the screen. (Refer to figure 2.1 if your Mac's not on.) The first menu is the **Apple** menu (the one with the symbol), followed by the **File**, **Edit**, **View**, **Label**, and **Special** menus. All Macs have these, so get used to seeing them.

You'll get to play with each of these menus later on (some in this chapter, some in chapter 7), but for now I want to simply introduce you to them so you know generally why they're on your Mac.

The Apple Menu

Click and hold on the small apple icon at the left edge of the menu bar. The menu that opens is the **Apple** menu. This

note
In case you don't remember, all the menu choices and menu commands in this book are bolded. This is supposed to make it easier for you to follow along. (You are following along, aren't you?)

menu is customizable; you can put anything you want into it (and in chapter 7, I'll show you how). The Apple menu is there no matter what you're doing: word processing, drawing, juggling numbers, whatever.

The File Menu

Every program has one of these, and all of them do roughly the same thing—help you do filing-type things to documents. **File** menus typically include commands that let you open existing documents, make new ones, print them, save them, and close them. Click on the **File** menu and take a look.

The Edit Menu

Now, on to the **Edit** menu. This is a great menu. All programs have one. You'll learn all about the **Edit** menu in chapter 3, but here's a preview: this menu lets you move things around in your documents (via a very cool technique called "cut and paste") and it enables you to undo mistakes.

GENIUS TIP

Those who master the Edit menu will have wonderful lives. Pay close attention to the section dealing with copying, cutting, and pasting in chapter 3.

The View Menu

This menu only appears in the Finder (the program that automatically runs when you turn on your Mac), but don't let that fool you into thinking it's not important. The **View** menu, as much as anything else, can make your Mac a nicer machine to use. Here's why.

The **View** menu lets you change the way that contents of windows are displayed (sorted alphabetically, sorted chronologically, displayed as groups of large or small icons, and other ways as well). You still don't know what a window is, but you will soon—and when you do, you'll get to play with the **View** menu and see how it works.

The Label Menu

A colossal waste of time and space. Thankfully, it appears only in the Finder and nowhere else.

The **Label** menu lets you "label" an icon with a color and a description—supposedly, you'd make all icons associated with Project A blue, and all those associated with Project B red. In practice, what really happens is we colorize our icons however we want to, just to make them look nice. It's certainly easy enough: click once on an icon, then choose a color from the **Label** menu. Trust me: If you actually use this menu for anything more than aesthetics you're the only one.

Watch out for that Erase Disk... command in the Special menu. It does just what you think it does.

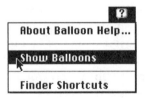

Balloon Help was supposed to be a big deal, but it hasn't turned out that way. Some programs don't offer Balloon Help; others offer it in a very limited fashion. Still, it's worth knowing how it works.

The Special Menu

You've seen this before: it's the one with **Restart** and **Shut Down**. You won't see it anywhere but in the Finder, which means you have to be able to get to the Finder in order to do these things. You'll learn how to get there in a few more pages.

So far, so good. No surprises here. But there are two more menus to deal with, and they're a little weird.

The Balloon Help Menu

The **Balloon Help** menu is under the question mark. Balloon Help is a kind of on-screen manual that helps you figure out what things are and to some degree, how to use them, without opening a real manual. Here's how to use it.

1. Click on the **Balloon Help** menu and drag down to **Show Balloons** (figure 2.24).

   You've just turned Balloon Help on.

```
              [ ? ]
   About Balloon Help...
  ▶Show Balloons
  ─────────────────────
   Finder Shortcuts
```

Figure 2.24
Turning on Balloon Help

2. Move the cursor until it points to the Trash.

You'll see a message like figure 2.25.

Figure 2.25
After pointing to the Trash

3. Move the cursor to the hard disk icon.

You'll see another message, like figure 2.26.

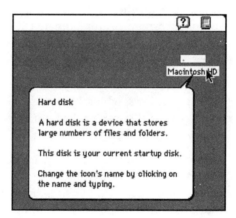

Figure 2.26
After pointing to the hard disk

4. Select a menu item and you'll get another message.

Figure 2.27 shows one possibility (it also shows you how to turn Balloon Help off).

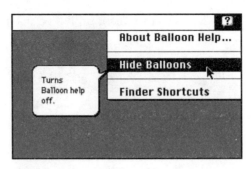

Figure 2.27
Turning Balloon Help off

The Application Menu

Last, but certainly not least, we come to the **Application** menu. This is a tough one. For some reason or another, beginners have a tough time understanding this menu. You're going to be different. I can sense it.

Think back to when you learned about applications. They're computer programs, remember? Different programs let you do different things, and miracle of miracles, your Mac lets you do more than one thing at a time. That's the good news.

The bad news is that each program has its own menu bar (and its own windows, which I *promise* to explain to you in just a few more pages). It doesn't take long before your Mac can become a mess.

Take a look at figure 2.28. Notice that picture just to the right of the **Balloon Help** menu? That's the **Application** menu. The picture at the top of the menu changes to reflect the program that's currently being used; in figure 2.28, it looks like a little Mac because that's the icon for the Finder.

The rest of the **Application** menu changes as you open programs. Figure 2.29 shows how it looks right after starting up; figure 2.30 shows how it looks after opening a word processor.

Application menu

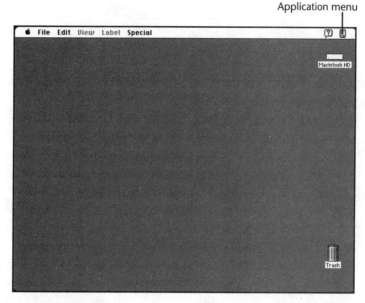

Figure 2.28
The familiar Desktop—notice the Application menu.

Figure 2.29
Application menu after starting up

Figure 2.30
Application menu after opening a word processor

Launch another application (maybe an address book, or a drawing program, or both) and the **Application** menu looks like figure 2.31.

Figure 2.31
Application menu after opening two more programs

Frankly, the Mac's become a mess, and it's hard to switch among the open applications. Unless, you know how to use the **Application** menu, that is!

Switching from program to program is as easy as selecting the one you want from the **Application** menu. (Again, only the currently running programs are in the menu.) Better than switching, though, is using the **Application** menu to tidy things up.

Suppose you've opened a word processor, a drawing program, and an address book. Your screen's going to look something like figure 2.32.

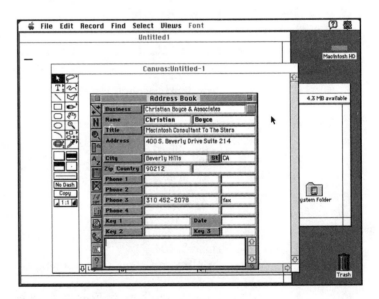

Figure 2.32
Ooh, what a mess

Suppose you'd like to focus on the address book. It would be nice if you could throw an electronic table cloth over everything else, wouldn't it? You can, by choosing **Hide Others** from the menu. Figure 2.33 shows what to choose, and figure 2.34 shows what it does.

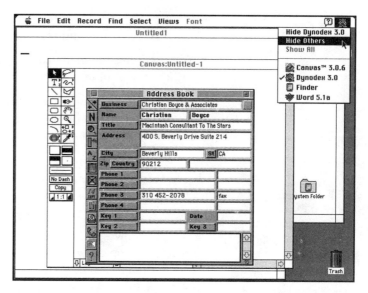

Figure 2.33
Choosing Hide Others

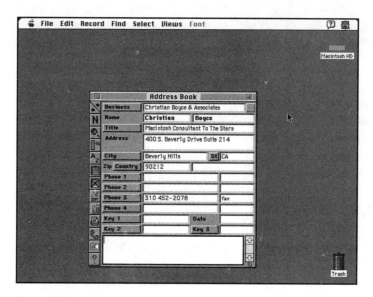

Figure 2.34
After choosing Hide Others

That does it for our menu overview. You'll get lots of menu practice throughout the book—sometimes more than you can stand—but it's good to have an idea of what menus are and what they can do, to begin with. Just remember:

- The **Apple** menu is customizable.

- Every program has a **File** menu, an **Edit** menu, a **Balloon Help** menu, and an **Application** menu.

- You don't need to memorize anything. Just be able to recognize commands when you see them.

Onward, Christian's Soldiers. Onward to windows, those things I've promised to explain for such a long time. The time has come. Let's do windows.

About Windows

Windows are a big deal on Macs. You write letters in word processing windows. You juggle numbers in spreadsheet program windows. You draw pictures in drawing program windows. Lots of other things get done in windows, too. (No, I'm not really sure why they're called windows. No one else seems to be, either. We're stuck with the term, so we may as well get used to it.)

Figure 2.35 shows a Macintosh window with every part labeled. Most windows—whether word processing, spreadsheet, drawing, or something else—have most of these parts. The things you learn here and now will help you in everything you do. Mark figure 2.35 (you'll need to find it for reference), then let's roll.

(The following exercises will teach you to work with windows. You've simply got to learn this stuff, so please please *please* turn on your Mac and try.)

1. *Double-click* on your hard disk icon (nice shortcut, eh?).

   Your hard disk opens, and you're looking at a *window*. Notice, by the way, that it looks a lot like figure 2.35. If it doesn't, it probably looks a lot like figure 2.36. We'll fix that in step 2.

n O t E *Windows, you say? Isn't that a PC program from Microsoft? Well, yes. But Macs had windows first. In fact, there's never been a Mac that didn't have windows. You'd think from the hype that Microsoft Windows for the PC was a major piece of original thinking, but it isn't. (The windows on the Mac aren't so original either. The basic idea came from Xerox. This didn't prevent Apple from trying to sue Microsoft's mice off when Windows for the PC became a runaway money maker.)*

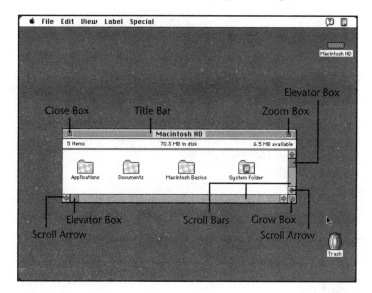

Figure 2.35
Basic Macintosh window

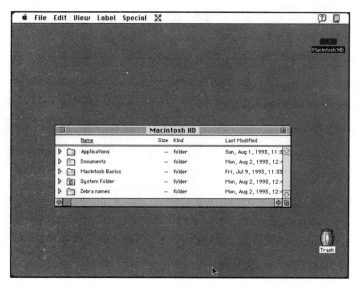

Figure 2.36
Not listed by icon

GENIUS TIP

Notice that the name of the icon is written across the top of the window. This makes it easy to remember where the window came from. In figures 2.35 and 2.36 it's clear that the window came from something called "Macintosh HD."

If you rename the icon while the window is open, you'll see the name change in the window title, too. No, you can't do it the other way around (you can't click on a window title and change its name there).

2. Choose **By Icon** from the **View** menu.

   Now your window looks like figure 2.35.

You've probably made this association already, but I'm paid by the word, so here goes: every window comes from somewhere. The windows in figures 2.35 and 2.36 came from hard disk icons. Double-clicking an icon opens up the icon; its contents are displayed in a window.

You can have several windows open if you wish. Many times, you'll wish. The key to working with multiple windows is good window management. The following examples will show you what you need to know.

1. Click on the window's *title bar* (refer to figure 2.35) and *drag* the window toward the upper left-hand corner of the screen.

   Figure 2.37 shows how your screen should look when you're done.

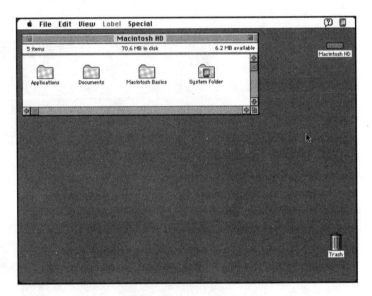

Figure 2.37
Window at top left-hand corner

You've just learned how to move a window. You'll move windows the same way from now until Apple invents something else. Remember: title bars are made for grabbing and moving.

2. Drag the window's *grow box* (see figure 2.35 again) down and to the left. Make the window cover about a quarter of the screen, as seen in figure 2.38.

n *The Mac won't let you*
O *drag things completely*
t *off the screen. If you*
E *try to move a window's*
title bar too far up, or
too far left, the window
will snap back to where
it started. If this hap-
pens to you, don't worry
about it; next time,
don't move the window
so far.

Take a look at the File menu (figure 2.39). See those strange-looking clover symbols paired with letters on the right? The strange-looking clover symbols represent the Command key, and the Command key/letter pairings are Command key shortcuts. Using a Command key shortcut is as easy as holding the Command key down while you press the appropriate letter. When you use a Command key shortcut, you've done exactly what you would have done had you selected the item from the menu.

You've just learned to *resize* a window. You'll resize windows the same way from now on.

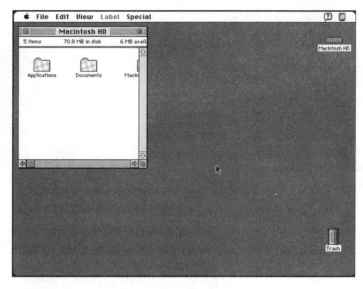

Figure 2.38
Window, stretched down and to the left

3. Make a new folder and name it Rosebud.

I assume you're getting good at making folders and don't need directions any more, but here's a hint: Look for the **New Folder** command (figure 2.39).

File
New Folder ⌘N
Open ⌘O
Print ⌘P
Close Window ⌘W
Get Info ⌘I
Sharing...
Duplicate ⌘D
Make Alias
Put Away ⌘Y
Find... ⌘F
Find Again ⌘G
Page Setup...
Print Desktop...

Figure 2.39
New Folder command

4. Double-click on the Rosebud folder.

It flies open and overlaps the first window. Figure 2.40 shows how it looks.

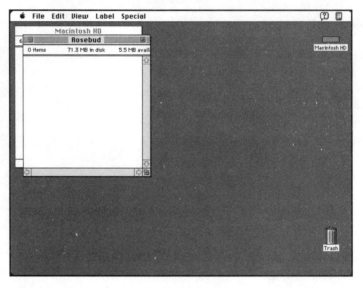

Figure 2.40
Second window overlapping the first

5. Click any place on the hard disk window (the one in the back). There's not much showing, but you don't need much; just get the tip of the arrow over that window, and click.

The window you clicked should come to the front, as seen in figure 2.41.

You've just learned how to bring a window to the front. There's no shortcut, but it's pretty easy as is. Remember: you need only to click on a window to bring it to the front. Try switching the windows back and forth by clicking on them now.

Drag the front window's title bar to the right, until it no longer overlaps the other window (figure 2.42). Now, can you tell which window's in the front? Of course you can. Just look for the one with the stripes in the title bar. And why is this important? Because if you happen to choose **New Folder** now, you'll want that folder to land in the proper window. Guess where that folder's going to land. Yup, it lands in the frontmost, or *active,* window.

n
o
t
E

Notice, by the way, that a window's title bar changes every time you bring it to the front. Specifically, the title bar becomes striped, and shows a box at each end. (If you had ten windows open, only one would have stripes and boxes in the title bar. Only one can be in the front, and that one gets the stripes.)

You might think that it's pretty obvious which window's in the front, since it covers up everything else, but that's not always the case. You'll see what I mean in a minute.

mAC LiNGO

The window that is on top is called the "active" window. Active also applies to the program in use. For example, if a Word window on top, Word is the active application.

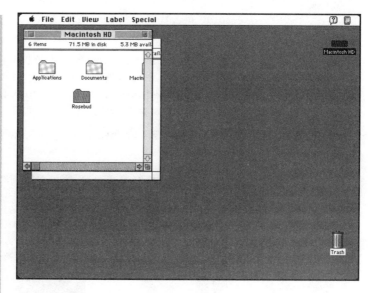

Figure 2.41
Windows, after clicking on the one in the rear

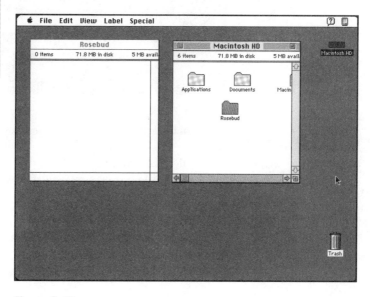

Figure 2.42
Two windows, not overlapping

As you can see, moving windows around isn't very hard. Sometimes, though, it's easier to temporarily *zoom* them to a large size, then *de-zoom* them back to a smaller size. This next exercise will show you how it works. Try this:

1. Resize the hard disk window by dragging the grow box up and to the left. (You might have to bring the hard disk window to the front by clicking on it first.) Make the window as small as it will get.

   Figure 2.43 shows how it looks when you're done.

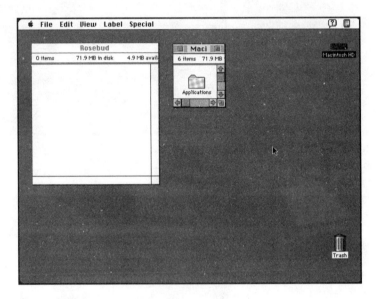

Figure 2.43
One small window, one larger one

n o t E *It looks like there are two boxes in the right-hand corner of the hard disk's title bar, and in fact there are. However, they're both parts of the same zoom box, and it's the big box that defines the zoom box's boundary. Click anywhere within the big box and you'll get the zooming effect.*

2. Click the *zoom box* in the right-hand corner of the hard disk's title bar (figure 2.44 shows a zoom box in a larger title bar).

   The window expands, as if you'd resized it yourself. Figure 2.45 shows how things look after zooming.

Figure 2.44
The zoom box

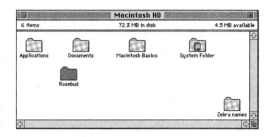

Figure 2.45
Zoomed hard disk window

When you first click on a zoom box, your Mac tries to make the window big enough to show everything in it. If it can do that without covering the Trash and hard disk icons, it will; otherwise, it gets as big as possible without covering up the Trash and hard drive icons.

TAKE COMMAND

There's more than one way to skin a cat. Figure 2.46 shows the File menu and the Close Window command. Note the Command-W shortcut. It'll make more sense if you think of it as "Close Window" and not just "Close."

3. Click on the zoom box again.

   The window flies back to the size you'd made it before. Subsequent zoom box clicks will toggle between "your" size and the Mac's size. Try it and see.

4. Now click on the box at the other (left) end of the title bar.

   The window closes.

   You just learned to close a window. The thing you clicked was the *close box*. Notice that the other window remains open—only the window you clicked on gets closed. You could have also used the **Close Window** command (figure 2.46).

Figure 2.46
Close Window command

5. Use Command-W (hold the Command key and press W) to close the remaining window.

Now that you know a shortcut for closing windows, let's open a bunch of them and let you have some practice. Let's open a lot of windows. Really make a mess.

1. Double-click on the hard disk again.

   The window opens.

2. Double-click on every *folder* icon you can find in the hard disk window. You'll have to click on the hard disk window, or double-click on the hard disk icon, if your hard disk window becomes hidden. Your desktop, when you're done, should look something like figure 2.47.

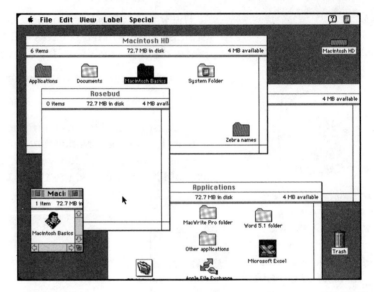

Figure 2.47
A big mess

If you wanted to close the windows, you *could* click on the close box of one, then the next, then the next, and so on. It could take a while. You could also use the Command-W shortcut and close the windows, again one by one. Naturally, there's a better way to do things, or I wouldn't have led you down this path:

3. Hold the Option key down (it's near the Command key), and click on the active window's close box. Figure 2.48 shows how to do it (my active window might be different than yours, look for the stripes).

Hold Option key and click here ——

Figure 2.48
Option-click on the close box

Nice move, eh? You bet it is. Your friends will gasp in admiration.

One more thing to show you.

1. Double-click on your hard disk icon.

2. Use the grow box to make the window very small.

    Figure 2.49 shows how it should look.

Figure 2.49
Very small window

3. Click on the zoom box to expand the window.

    See all the stuff in it? Figure 2.50 shows the zoomed window.

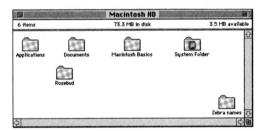

Figure 2.50
The zoomed window

4. Click on the zoom box again to shrink the window to its very small size.

Scroll bar arrows seem to work backward: Click on the down arrow and the icons move up; click on the up arrow and the icons move down. It seems backward to everyone at first.

However, think of it this way: You've got more stuff than can fit in a window. When you want to see the stuff at the bottom, click on the down arrow. When you want to see the stuff at the top, click on the up arrow. Simple.

Notice that the window is bordered by gray bars across the bottom and on the right (figure 2.51). These bars are called *scroll bars*.

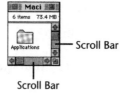

Scroll Bar

Scroll Bar

Figure 2.51
Window with scroll bars

5. Click on the arrow indicated in figure 2.52.

    You'll see something happen. Click again and it will happen again.

Click here

Figure 2.52
Clicking the down arrow

The *something* that happened is that the icons in the window slid up. Officially, the *something* is called *scrolling a window*. Most Macintosh windows have scroll bars; most have up and down arrows (and most have left and right arrows, as well).

6. Click on the up arrow.

    The window scrolls up (or, if you like, the icons slide down). Try clicking and holding the mouse button down rather than clicking and letting go. It's a whole lot faster.

Take another look at figure 2.51. Those squares in the scroll bars are *elevator boxes*. You may have noticed them moving up and down as you clicked the scroll arrows (if you haven't, click on those scroll arrows again and keep an eye peeled for the elevator boxes).

> **n**
> **O**
> **t**
> **E**
> *Remember, all windows work the same way, whether you're writing a letter, playing with numbers, or doing whatever. This drag-the-box approach will work no matter what. If, for example, you're working on a twenty-page word processing document (perhaps a list of people to send a copy of this book to), you'll get to the bottom in a hurry by dragging the elevator box. Clicking the scroll bar's down arrow will take much longer.*
>
> *By the way: if you drag the elevator box to the middle of the scroll bar, you'll be at (or near) the middle of the document, or in the example above, page ten.*

An elevator box at the top of the scroll bar means you're as high as you can go (thus, there's no reason to continue clicking the scroll bar's up arrow). An elevator box at the bottom of the scroll bar means you're as low as you can go (thus, there's not reason to continue clicking the scroll bar's down arrow). An elevator box in the middle of the scroll bar means you're somewhere in between; there's more to see by going up, and there's more to see by going down. Here's the cool part: You can move the elevator box directly, like so:

1. Click on the vertical elevator box (the one in the scroll bar on the right). Hold the mouse button down.

2. Drag the box to the bottom of the scroll bar (if it's already there, drag it to the top).

This technique takes you straight to the bottom (or straight to the top) of a window in a hurry. This maneuver will save you countless mouse clicks.

One last thing to know about elevator boxes: they only show up when there's something to scroll. When a window's big enough to show everything, the elevator boxes disappear (and the scroll bars turn white). You should convince yourself of this:

1. Click on the zoom box of the hard disk window. Did the elevator boxes disappear? They should have.

2. Click on the zoom box again. Did the elevator boxes come back? They should have. Figure 2.53 shows how it looks.

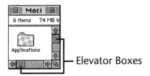 — Elevator Boxes

Figure 2.53
Window with elevator boxes

And that, my friend, is all you need to know about windows. Every program uses windows, and every window looks and behaves more or less like the ones you worked with in this chapter. Couple your window expertise with what you know about icons and menus, and I'd say you're ready to make some documents.

GENIUS TIP

That gray area in the scroll bars has a name; it's called, believe it or not, the gray area. Clicking in it scrolls the window a window-full at a time—upward if you click above the elevator box, downward if you click below the elevator box. This makes scrolling through large documents easy: you click in the gray area, under the elevator box, and skip down a window at a time. Try it—it beats scrolling a line at a time, which is what you're doing when you click on a scroll arrow.

note

Do yourself a big favor now and take that Macintosh Basics tour. Look for a folder called Macintosh Basics on your hard disk, open it up, and double-click on the Macintosh Basics icon inside.

If you don't have a copy of the tour, re-read this chapter. You need to master this stuff before moving on.

That's what you'll do in the next two chapters. But first, your quiz:

1. What is a "wire head?"

2. Are you absolutely positive that you know the difference between applications, documents, and folders?

3. Have you taken the *free* guided tour of the Macintosh called "Macintosh Basics?" It probably came with your Mac in a folder called "Macintosh Basics."

4. How many System Folders do you have? How many should you have?

5. Do you know two ways to make a new folder?

6. Does the Mac ever run out of folders?

7. Can you rename folders with ease?

8. Can you retrieve items mistakenly tossed in the Trash? Is there a statute of limitations?

9. Can you move items into and out of folders and disks?

10. Do you understand the difference between copying and moving?

11. Do you know how to get a floppy disk out of your Mac?

12. Do you know how to use the **Application** menu?

13. Can you identify the parts of the window shown in figure 2.54 without cheating?

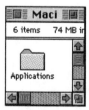

Figure 2.54
A typical window

14. Can you move windows and resize them?

15. Can you bring the window you want to the front?

16. Do you know the significance of The Cross of Saint Hans?

17. Do you care?

Chapter 3
How to Use a Word Processor

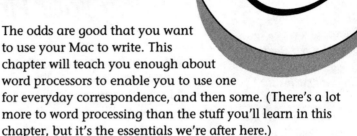

The odds are good that you want
to use your Mac to write. This
chapter will teach you enough about
word processors to enable you to use one
for everyday correspondence, and then some. (There's a lot
more to word processing than the stuff you'll learn in this
chapter, but it's the essentials we're after here.)

When you're through with this chapter, you'll have written a
letter, saved it, changed it, and printed it. What more could you
possibly need?

What's a Word Processor, and Do I Have One?

Ah. Good questions. Word processors, as mentioned earlier, are
computer programs used for writing. In effect, they turn
Macintoshes into high-powered typewriters that are unbeliev-
ably forgiving and that have options galore.

Now, do you have one? Well, if you bought something called
"Microsoft Word" or "MacWrite" or something ending in the
word "Works," you do. If you're not sure, look for an icon
matching any of those shown in figure 3.1.

These are not the only word processors in the world, just some
of the common ones. If you can't find one of them, check for
anything with the word "word" in the title, such as
"WordPerfect."

ClarisWorks MacWrite Pro TeachText Word 5.1a

Figure 3.1
Word processor icons

Creating Your First Letter

Assuming you can find a word processor icon, double-click on it and watch the fun. If you're using Microsoft Word version 5.1, you'll get a combination welcome, warning, and advertisement from Microsoft, and then a blank piece of electronic paper, ready for you to fill with words (figure 3.2). If you happen to be using any of the products ending with the word "Works" (the wonderful ClarisWorks, the not-bad Great Works, or the totally doggy Microsoft Works), you'll have to take an intermediate step that tells the program that you want to work on a word processing document and not something else. This step involves clicking on a button labeled "Word Processing"; I'm certain you can do it.

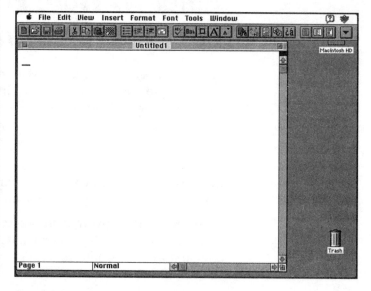

Figure 3.2
Blank page in Microsoft Word 5.1a

GENIUS TIP

Macintosh applications are upgraded roughly every year. You have to keep paying money to the company that made the program if you want to stay up-to-date. Generally, higher numbers mean newer versions. Although the companies want you to upgrade to every version, you shouldn't do so until you're sure that the new version has something to offer that is worth the upgrade fee.

That small, flashing, vertical line is the "insertion point". It shows where the next thing you type will appear. All word processors (and most text functions in other programs) use insertion points.

Notice anything familiar? How about that window? Look at all these features you already know:

- Title bar
- Close box
- Zoom box
- Scroll bars, scroll arrows, and elevator boxes
- Grow box

Incredible. Just as I told you. Maybe you'll believe me from now on.

Let's poke around a little and see what the program can do.

1. Type `Dear Christian:`

   Miracle of miracles, what you type appears on the screen. If you make a mistake, don't sweat it. You'll learn how to fix mistakes later.

2. Press the Return key three times.

   Notice that a small, flashing, vertical line moves down one line every time you press the key.

3. Type the paragraph shown in figure 3.3. Don't press Return, not even once.

   The Mac will wrap the words around to the beginning of a new line when it needs to. This feature alone makes a word processor far superior to a typewriter. Now you can focus on writing and not on the bell at the end of the line. As before, don't worry about mistakes.

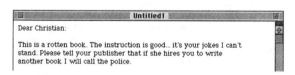

Figure 3.3
A practice paragraph

Now, let's add a paragraph and sign off.

4. Press Return two times.

   The insertion point jumps down two lines.

5. Type the paragraph shown in figure 3.4. Again, don't press Return even once. Let the Mac handle things for you. And again, if you make mistakes, leave them there.

While you're at it, tell your publisher I want my money back. The sooner the better. I'll have you know that I am an attorney... if I find a lawyer joke in here, I'll sue|

Figure 3.4
Second practice paragraph

6. Press Return two times and type your name.

Your screen should look a lot like the one shown in figure 3.5.

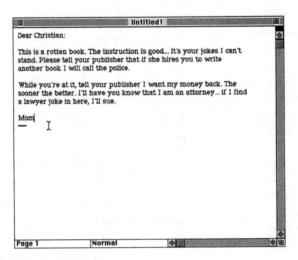

Figure 3.5
Your letter (draft 1)

That wasn't so hard, was it? You've actually written a letter using a word processor! Before you invite the neighbors over to show off, let's save your letter so it's stored for all time (or at least until you throw it into the Trash). This is an important step and you'll do it the same way in every program.

1. Choose **Save** from the **File** menu.

You get a dialog box (remember that term?) looking something like the one shown in figure 3.6. Don't worry if you see something slightly different—each application modifies this dialog box to suit its needs.

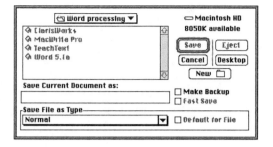

Figure 3.6
Save As... dialog box

2. Type Letter to CB.

3. Click on the Save button (figure 3.7).

   The dialog box goes away and you're back at your letter.

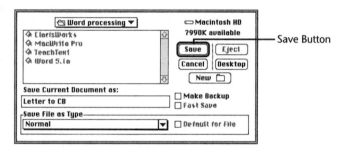

Figure 3.7
The Save button

Look at figure 3.7 again. Each one of those rounded-corner rectangles is a button. Each button is generally referred to by the word inside the rounded-corner rectangle, as in "the Save button," "the Cancel button," and so on. You'll be clicking on buttons frequently.

Notice that your letter's title bar, which used to say "Untitled1" or something similar, now says "Letter to CB." This is a clue that you have saved this document at least once. It's also a clue to which document you're working on. Right now there's just one document on-screen, but most programs let you work on two or three or more documents at once, and it's good to know which one you're working on.

Let's quit writing and break for coffee; choose **Quit** from the **File** menu (figure 3.8).

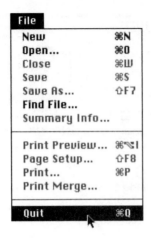

Figure 3.8
Choosing Quit from the File menu

The word processor goes away and you're back at the desktop. Look for your letter in the window occupied by the application that you used to create it; it should be easy to spot. Figure 3.9 shows what the letter's icon looks like if you are using Microsoft Word.

Figure 3.9
"Letter to CB" icon

Now go get that coffee. It's good for you.

Making Changes

Had enough coffee? Great. Let's say you've thought things over and want to make a few changes to your letter. No problem:

1. Double-click on the letter's icon.

   The letter knows which application created it and assumes you'll use the same application for editing, so it launches that application. Your letter appears on the screen, just as you left it.

The keys with the arrows on them are called "cursor keys." You ought to try them, especially if you are allergic to mice.

2. Find the word *rotten* in the opening paragraph. Let's change it to something less severe, like *lousy*.

3. Move the pointer around until the I-beam cursor is just to the right of the *n* in *rotten*. Use the keys with the arrows on them if you'd rather.

4. Click once (you won't have to do this if you moved the insertion point via cursor keys). The insertion point should be just to the right of the *n* (figure 3.10); if it isn't, move the mouse around and try clicking again (or use the cursor keys).

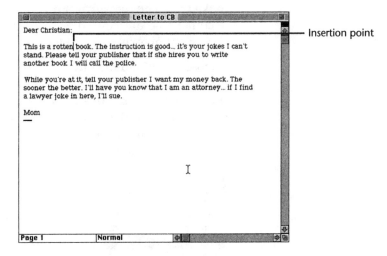

Figure 3.10
Insertion point just to the right of *rotten*

Look around your keyboard for a key labeled Delete or Backspace. You'll need it for the next step.

5. Press the Delete key (or the Backspace key, if that's what your keyboard has).

Notice anything? You should. Pressing Delete eats up the character directly to the left of the insertion point. You might not have noticed anything because that character might have been a space, but you'll notice something this time.

6. Press the Delete key again, and again and again and again and again.

If we both counted correctly, the entire "rotten" word should be gone. (If not, one more Delete ought to do it.)

7. Type the word lousy.

   Notice that the characters you type appear directly to the left of the insertion point.

Downright easy, isn't it? Making changes is really a matter of clicking in the right place. See if you can change the line, "I want my money back" to "I want my money back, times two." Scan your letter for typos and fix them using the "click, delete if necessary, and type" technique. Report here when you're done.

Ready? Cool. This editing of yours is very impressive. So impressive that you ought to save your work (if you don't, you'll get to make those changes all over again the next time you open this document, because they aren't stored until you say so). This will be easy for an experienced Mac user such as yourself.

Choose **Save** from the **File** menu (figure 3.11). Notice that you did *not* get a dialog box. That's because you've already named this document. Once a document is saved, subsequent saves delete the old version and replace it with the new one. Be sure you understand this: *your old version is history as soon as you make changes and save them. Only the new version remains.*

File	
New	⌘N
Open...	⌘O
Close	⌘W
Save	⌘S
Save As...	⇧F7
Find File...	
Summary Info...	
Print Preview...	⌘⌥I
Page Setup...	⇧F8
Print...	⌘P
Print Merge...	
Quit	⌘Q

Figure 3.11
Choosing Save from the File menu

Let's dress the letter up. Give it some pizzazz.

1. Click just before the *D* in *Dear*, and keep the mouse button down.

2. Move the mouse (while holding the mouse button down, you know, drag, man!) to the right until the entire first line is highlighted (figure 3.12).

Next time you save, try the Command key shortcut, Command-S. You can see it listed in the File menu, shown in figure 3.11. Command-S is a standard shortcut and almost every program uses it for the Save command. Get in the habit of hitting Command-S every time you take a break. Like now.

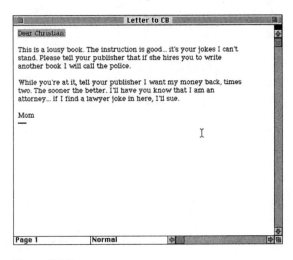

Figure 3.12
Highlighted first line

(Remember learning that the key to using a Mac was selecting a subject, then doing something to it? You've just selected the first line of the letter as your subject.)

3. Choose any font from the **Font** menu (figure 3.13).

The selected text is changed (figure 3.14) to the font you selected.

The word "font" means "typeface."

Figure 3.13
Choosing a font from the Font menu

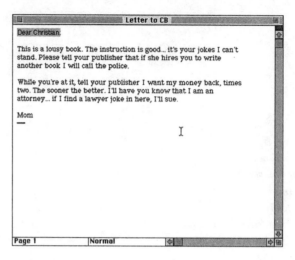

Figure 3.14
After changing fonts

Notice that the text remains highlighted; this means we can make more changes to it. Let's make it bigger:

Choose a font size from the **Font** menu (figure 3.15). Some word processors have a separate **Size** menu; you may need to choose from that if you're not using Word. Figure 3.16 shows what you get if you choose 24-point.

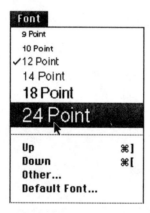

Figure 3.15
Choosing a size

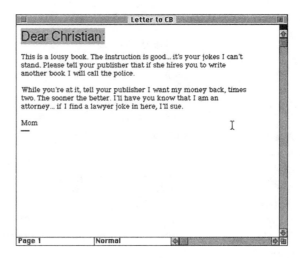

Figure 3.16
After choosing 24-point

n *Type sizes are mea-*
o *sured in points. The*
t *text of your standard*
E *business letter is 12-*
point type. Seventy-two-
point text is an inch
tall, more or less.

Now suppose we make that first line bold. That's easy, too:

1. Choose **Bold** from the **Format** menu (you'll find **Bold** in the **Style** menu in some other word processors).

   Figure 3.17 shows what you're looking for. Notice that there are a bunch of other styles to choose from (underline, italic, and so on). Notice also that your text becomes bold.

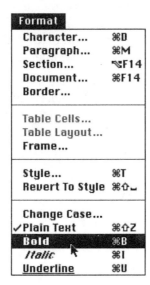

Many applications use
Command-B as the shortcut
for Bold.

Figure 3.17
Choosing Bold from the Format menu

You may have noticed that when you pull down menus like Font and Format, certain items have a checkmark by them (for example, Plain Text in figure 3.17). These checkmarks show you what is currently applied to wherever the cursor is or to what you have selected (highlighted). Thus, if you go to the Font menu and see a checkmark by Helvetica, that means that Helvetica is the current font. This can be very handy when you're not sure what you've got.

2. Choose **Bold** again.

   Notice that your text became "unbold." That's how it works: bold on, bold off. Choose it again and it's bold on again.

Pretty easy, eh? As long as you don't click anywhere else, that first line of text will remain selected, letting you experiment with fonts and sizes and styles all the live-long day.

Getting Out of Trouble

Ever wish you could take back something you said? "I'll take care of your cat while you're on vacation" stands out for me. If real life were like a Macintosh, you'd choose **Undo** from the **Edit** menu and say something else. (I'd choose **Undo** and mention a sudden allergy.)

Seriously, the **Undo** command is a lifesaver. It undoes deletions, font changes, and nearly everything else you can do on a Mac. It's always under the **Edit** menu, it's always at the top, and it's always called **Undo**.

The **Undo** command has a single limitation, but it's a doozy: *you can only undo your very most recent action.* That's important, so I'll say it again: *you can only undo your very most recent action.* You ought to say this a couple of times yourself. Translated, **Undo**'s limitation means you can't tell your Mac to undo what you did half an hour ago, unless that was the last thing you did. You typically can't undo anything if you've saved your work, so watch out for that one, too.

Limitation or not, being able to undo gives you the power to experiment like crazy (one move at a time). You're only an **Undo** away from putting things back the way they used to be. Let's try it:

1. Select the first line of your letter (it will still be selected if you haven't clicked anywhere else yet).

2. Press the Delete key.

   The entire line is zapped.

3. Choose **Undo** from the **Edit** menu (figure 3.18).

   The text comes back!

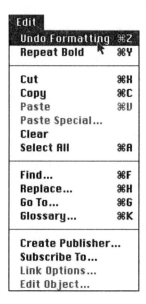

Figure 3.18
Choosing Undo from the Edit menu

Convinced that Undo is the key to carefree Mac work? Me, too. It's even handier when you use the command key shortcut, which happens to be Command-Z. Yes, Command-U would have made more sense, but that one was already taken for Underline. Every Mac application worth its salt follows the Command-Z convention for Undo so you might as well get used to using it.

If Command-Z doesn't undo anything, the odds are that there's nothing to undo. Some actions, like saving, printing, and erasing disks can't be undone, and your Mac knows it.

4. Choose **Undo** a second time.

    The text goes away again!

Three guesses as to what happens when you choose **Undo** a third time. (Give up? Try it.) Think about it: first, you undo the deletion; then, you undo the Undo; finally, you undo the Undo that undid the first Undo. Easier done than said.

Want to show off? Try selecting all the text in your letter (Command-A will do it, or you can drag from beginning to end) and press Delete. *Everything disappears*. Now press Command-Z to undo your deletion. *Everything comes back*. This is a great stunt to pull at work, especially on an important document with your boss looking over your shoulder. The longer you wait to press Command-Z the more the boss will hyperventilate.

I'd say it's time to save your work. Remember, Command-S. Now, let's print.

Printing

Assuming you have a printer connected to your Macintosh, and assuming you've switched it on, you're ready to print. If you don't have a printer, go get one, and if you have one but it's not switched on, switch it on. Moving forward:

1. Choose **Print...** from the **File** menu (figure 3.19).

   You'll see a dialog box like the one shown in figure 3.20.

File	
New	⌘N
Open...	⌘O
Close	⌘W
Save	⌘S
Save As...	⇧F7
Find File...	
Summary Info...	
Print Preview...	⌘⌥I
Page Setup...	⇧F8
Print...	⌘P
Print Merge...	
Quit	⌘Q

Figure 3.19
Choosing **Print**... from the **File** menu

```
Printer: "LaserWriter IIf"                    8.0    [ Print ]
Copies: [1]  Pages: ⦿ All  ○ From: [    ] To: [    ]  [ Cancel ]
┌Paper Source─────────────┐  ┌Destination──┐
│⦿ All ○ First from: [Cassette ▼]│  │⦿ Printer    │  [ Options ]
│       Remaining from: [Cassette ▼]│  │○ File       │  [ Help ]
└─────────────────────────┘  └─────────────┘

Print Pages:  ⦿ All  ○ Odd Pages Only   ○ Even Pages Only
Section Range: From: 1   To: 1     □ Print Selection Only
□ Print Hidden Text  □ Print Next File  □ Print Back To Front
```

Figure 3.20
Print Dialog Box

Some Print dialog boxes are slightly different than the one in figure 3.20, but not by much. The most important parts of any print dialog box are:

• The Copies box, where you input the number of copies to print.

You may have noticed that some menu items have ellipses after them (such as Print... and Save As...), while others do not (for example, Save and Copy). Ellipses indicate that you will have some other choices to make after you select the item. Most of the time these choices will be made in a dialog box. If there are no ellipses after an item, the action you select will be performed immediately after you release the mouse button.

- The Pages area, where you select which pages (all or just some) to print.

- The Print button, which starts the printer.

  We'll print the whole thing. Notice that the Mac assumes you want one copy of the entire document without your choosing anything. This is standard behavior.

2. Press the Print button.

   With luck, your letter is printed. You can send it to me if you want (my address is printed in the back of the book).

Ready for more? Great. This last section shows you how to move words and paragraphs around and to speed the creation of repetitive documents—with very little typing.

Using Cut, Copy, and Paste

Cut, **Copy**, and **Paste** reside just underneath **Undo** in every **Edit** menu known to Mac. These are darned-near universal and where they aren't, they ought to be.

Like their real life counterparts (I'm talking about scissors and glue), **Cut**, **Copy**, and **Paste** let you rearrange things without starting over. Diligent application of **Cut**, **Copy**, and **Paste** techniques will let you follow "Boyce's Rule of Sloth," to wit:

Never type anything twice.

Let's put **Copy** and **Paste** through their paces. You'll learn about **Cut** a bit later.

Start by opening a new word processing document.

1. Choose **New** from the **File** menu.

   You'll get a new, blank document; notice that you didn't have to put away (close) your letter before opening another document.

2. Type the following:

   My Bonnie lies over the ocean (press Return)

   My Bonnie lies over the sea

In every application, the shortcut for Copy is always Command-C.

I assume you know what comes next (don't tell me you don't recognize the song!), and since you've dedicated your life to "Boyce's Rule of Sloth," this is an excellent opportunity to copy the first line and paste it after the second.

3. Click after the word *ocean* in the first line and drag left, just past the My.

   The whole first line should be highlighted.

4. Choose **Copy** from the **Edit** menu (figure 3.21).

   Nothing happens, at least nothing you can see. Behind the scenes, though, the first line's been copied.

Edit	
Undo Formatting	⌘Z
Repeat Bold	⌘Y
Cut	⌘H
Copy	⌘C
Paste	⌘U
Paste Special...	
Clear	
Select All	⌘A
Find...	⌘F
Replace...	⌘H
Go To...	⌘G
Glossary...	⌘K
Create Publisher...	
Subscribe To...	
Link Options...	
Edit Object...	

Figure 3.21
Choosing Copy from the Edit menu

5. Click after the word sea in the second line.

6. Press Return to knock the insertion point down one line.

7. Choose **Paste** from the **Edit** menu (figure 3.22). As if by magic, line three appears. Press Return and type the last line yourself.

Your screen shows the first verse in all its glory:

My Bonnie lies over the ocean

My Bonnie lies over the sea

My Bonnie lies over the ocean

Oh bring back my Bonnie to me

Edit	
Undo Copy	⌘Z
Repeat Bold	⌘Y
Cut	⌘H
Copy	⌘C
Paste	⌘U
Paste Special...	
Clear	
Select All	⌘A
Find...	⌘F
Replace...	⌘H
Go To...	⌘G
Glossary...	⌘K
Create Publisher...	
Subscribe To...	
Link Options...	
Edit Object...	

The shortcut for Paste is always Command-V (I'll explain why in a minute). Recall that the obvious choice, Command-P, was already taken by Print....

Figure 3.22
Choosing Paste from the Edit menu

Now the chorus. This will be impressive. Sing along if you wish. Campfire optional.

1. Press a couple of Returns, then type Bring back.

2. Drag through Bring back, and **Copy** it (**File** menu).

3. Press Return, then **Paste** the text; press Return again, and **Paste** again.

4. Type the rest of the third line of the chorus yourself, then press Return. Another couple of Pastes and Returns and you're practically done. Finish up, trying to type as little as possible.

Notice that you were able to paste two times even though you only copied once. In fact, you can paste as many times as you want without reloading a fresh copy of the text. With few exceptions, this is The Way of the Mac, and it is good.

The shortcut for Cut is Command-X. It is ever thus.

Notice, if you will, that the shortcuts for Undo, Cut, Copy, and Paste are Command-Z, -X, -C, and -V. Notice also that those keys are conveniently grouped on the bottom row of your keyboard.

The finished chorus:

```
Bring back

Bring back

Bring back my Bonnie to me, to me

Bring back

Bring back

Bring back my Bonnie to me
```

How about that! You hardly typed anything but you've written a whole song. That's what **Copy** and **Paste** are for. Let's do one more to learn about **Cut,** then we'll call it a day.

1. Select the chorus by dragging through it.

   The chorus should be highlighted.

2. Choose **Cut** from the **Edit** menu (figure 3.23).

   The chorus disappears. This disappearance is what differentiates **Cut** from **Copy**: **Copy** would have left the original text intact.

Edit	
Undo Copy	⌘Z
Repeat Bold	⌘Y
Cut	⌘H
Copy	⌘C
Paste	⌘U
Paste Special...	
Clear	
Select All	⌘A
Find...	⌘F
Replace...	⌘H
Go To...	⌘G
Glossary...	⌘K
Create Publisher...	
Subscribe To...	
Link Options...	
Edit Object...	

Figure 3.23
Choosing Cut from the Edit menu

3. Click at the very beginning of the document, to the left of the first My.

   The insertion point should be blinking away, showing where the stuff you're about to paste will go.

4. Choose **Paste** from the **Edit** menu, or do a Command-V.

   Your chorus appears at the top of the document. Granted, this hasn't improved things, but it created a great opportunity to practice **Undo**, so go ahead and try it. If you want to make things right, click at the end of the document and **Paste** the chorus where it belongs.

That's it. Let's Quit; choose **Quit** from the **File** menu. You get a dialog box asking if you want to save your changes. If you do, click on the appropriate button. If you don't, click on the other appropriate button. If you've changed your mind about quitting, click on Cancel.

Time for a quiz.

1. Which word processor do you use?

2. Do you know how to move the insertion point with the mouse? How about using cursor keys?

3. Can you change fonts, sizes, and styles?

4. Do you know how to save your work?

5. Can you use **Undo**?

6. Do you understand **Cut**, **Copy**, and **Paste**, and do you pledge to never type anything twice?

7. Have we met?

Chapter 4
How to Use a Spreadsheet Program

Anyone who works with numbers should know
how to use a spreadsheet program. The rest of you should learn
what spreadsheet programs are all about, partly because you
might need one someday and partly because you might need
one now and not know it.

This chapter explains the basics of creating a spreadsheet,
entering data, creating formulas, making changes, and printing. A mini-mini lesson on turning your spreadsheet data into
spiffy charts and graphs finishes things off.

What's a Spreadsheet Program, and Do I Have One?

Spreadsheet programs are to numbers what word processors are
to words. The documents they create (called *spreadsheets*) start
out looking like an electronic ledger pad (a grid formed out of
rows and columns). You type in your numbers and the spreadsheet, when properly set up, adds them up automatically. Or
figures percentages automatically. Or finds differences, or
maximums, or averages, all automatically. *Spreadsheet programs are good at math.*

Figure 4.1 shows the icon for Microsoft Excel 4.0, the most
popular Macintosh spreadsheet program and the one I'll use for
most of our examples. Be aware that Excel is so deep and full of
features that the manual comes in six parts. Yikes.

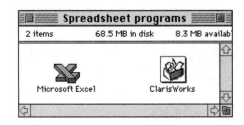

Figure 4.1
Spreadsheet program icons

Figure 4.1 also shows the icon for ClarisWorks 2.0, whose spreadsheet module (and manual) is kinder and gentler than Excel. Remember that the concepts learned here will help you in *any* spreadsheet program, not just Excel and ClarisWorks; if you're using Lotus 1-2-3 or Resolve or WingZ or whatever, the techniques shown in this chapter require only slight modification.

Creating Your First Spreadsheet

Let's get right into it. We'll make a spreadsheet to keep track of household bills, rearrange it, jazz it up, and print it.

Figure 4.2 shows what we're going to make: a neatly tabulated record of how much is owed to whom, and when. You can't tell by looking at the picture, but the total was calculated automatically.

	A	B	C	D	
1	Bills	Amount	Date Due		
2	Telephone	$122.56	1-Sep-93		
3	Electricity	$14.62	3-Sep-93		
4	Rent	$695.00	1-Sep-93		
5	VISA	$321.21	28-Aug-93		
6	Insurance	$245.36	19-Aug-93		
7	Cable TV	$11.95	15-Sep-93		
8					
9	Total	$1,410.70			
10				⇧	

Figure 4.2
The goal: a record of bills to pay

n
o *I enlarged the font*
t *used in my spread-*
E *sheet examples so that*
you could see what I
was doing. Your
spreadsheet will show
many more rows and
columns.

Here's how you do it. First, launch your spreadsheet program: double-click on the Excel icon (or the ClarisWorks icon, or whatever icon you have that belongs to a spreadsheet program). If you're using Excel, you'll get the same sort of combination welcome, advertisement, and stern warning about piracy that Microsoft's other products open with (figure 4.3), and then a blank spreadsheet (figure 4.4). All blank spreadsheets, regardless of origin, look pretty much like figure 4.4.

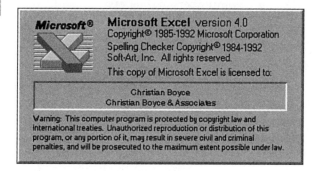

Figure 4.3
A friendly greeting from Microsoft

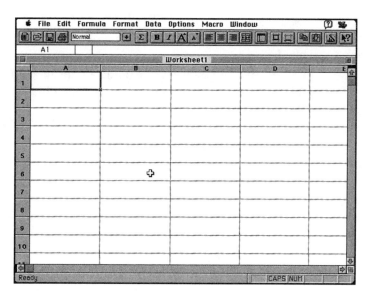

Figure 4.4
A blank spreadsheet

What a surprise: this window looks a lot like the windows you learned about in chapter 2! Hate to say I told you so, but just look at that title bar, zoom box, close box, grow box, blah, blah, blah. It's all there, just as I promised. Next time you'll trust me, right?

Notice that Excel has a toolbar across the top. Some spread-sheet programs do, some spreadsheet programs don't. What they *all* have is a grid of rows and columns designated by numbers and letters.

Let's type in the data. You can customize your spreadsheet to contain information for your own bills later. For now, do what I do:

1. Move the cursor (in Excel it looks like an inflated plus sign) until it is over cell A1.

2. Click.

   You should see a border around cell A1 now. (It might have been there already and probably was. No harm in being sure.)

3. Type the word Bills, then press Enter.

   The spreadsheet looks like the one shown in figure 4.5.

   I don't know why, but nearly everybody wants to press Return when I tell them to press Enter. If your spreadsheet looks like figure 4.6 instead of figure 4.5, you probably pressed Return instead of Enter.

A "cell" is just a box on a spreadsheet. The "A1" reference tells you that we're talking about the cell at the intersection of column A and row 1.

	A	B	C
1	Bills		
2			
3		✛	
4			
5			
6			
7			
8			
9			
10			

Figure 4.5
After entering the word *Bills*

A	B	C
Bills		
		✛

Figure 4.6
You pressed Return, didn't you?

GENIUS TIP

Suppose you type something into a cell and want to type something else into the cell to the right. The moron presses Enter to enter the stuff into the first cell, then presses Tab or the right arrow to move to the cell to the right. The total Mac genius skips the "press Enter" step and simply presses Tab. By some miracle (I have no idea how or why), this works. This shortcut works with arrow keys in all directions, the Return key, the Shift-Return, and the Shift-Tab as well. It'll cut your total keystrokes way down.

4. Click on cell B1 and type Amount. Press Enter.

5. Click on cell C1 and type Date Due. Press Enter.

This isn't very hard, is it? The most troublesome task so far is positioning the cursor over the proper cell and clicking. Even that's not very difficult, but it can be a hassle when you're working on a large spreadsheet. Fortunately, there are some easier ways to move around.

The cursor keys on your keyboard (the ones with the arrows on them) let you go up, down, left, and right without using the mouse. (This is particularly handy for trackball users.) Tap the keys or hold them down; a little experimentation is the ticket in this chapter.

Don't like the cursor keys? Then try the Tab key. Pressing Tab moves you one cell to the right. Holding Shift while pressing Tab moves you one cell to the left.

Want to move down? Press the Return key (you may have "experimented" with this already). Want to move up? Hold Shift and press Return. Nothing to it at all.

Piece of cake. Let's save the thing before something happens to end our session prematurely.

1. Choose **Save** from the **File** menu (figure 4.7).

   You'll get the Save As... dialog box shown in figure 4.8, and sure enough, it looks a lot like the one from Microsoft Word. Well, sort of.

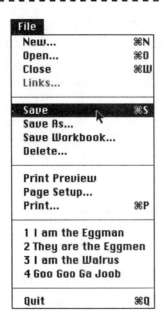

Figure 4.7
Choosing **Save** from the **File** menu

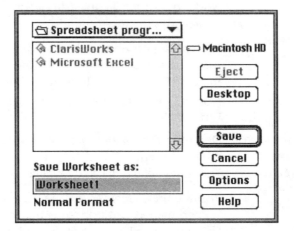

Figure 4.8
Save As... dialog box

As with Word, you don't have to choose **Save As...** to get the Save As... dialog box if you're saving your document for the first time. This is a nearly universal characteristic.

2. Type Bills and click on the Save button (figure 4.9).

After doing so, you'll see that "Bills" appears in the title bar.

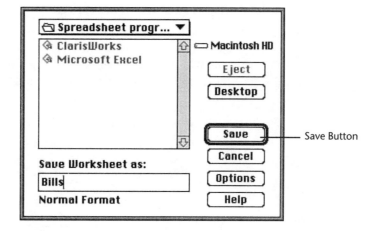

Figure 4.9
The Save button

Let's get back to entering our data, but this time let's make it go faster:

1. Click on cell A2 and hold the mouse button down.

2. Drag the mouse down until you're over cell A7.

3. Let go.

   Your spreadsheet should look like figure 4.10.

   What you've done is called *selecting a range of cells,* or simply *selecting a range.* Notice that one cell is white with a border while the others are black. The white one, called *the active cell,* is the one where stuff you type will go.

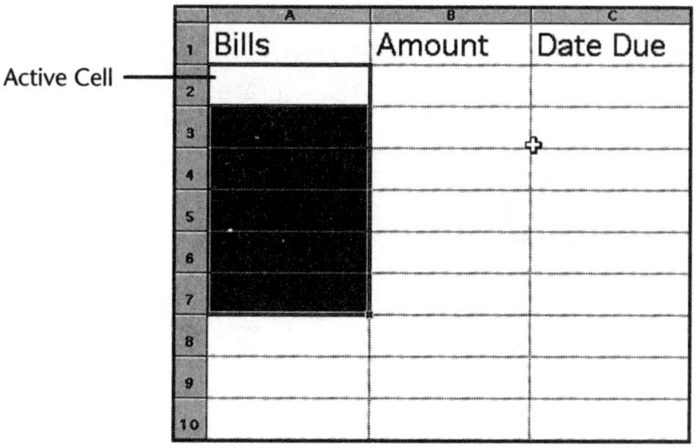

Figure 4.10
After selecting a range

And why does this make entering data go faster? Because you can type a word (or a number) and press Enter, or Tab, or Return, and the item will be entered into the cell and the active cell will move one cell down. Which means you can get into a data-entering groove in which you don't watch the screen, as follows:

1. Type Telephone.

2. Press Enter.

    The active cell moves down, ready for you to enter something into it (figure 4.11).

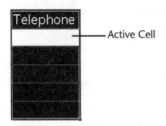

Figure 4.11
Active cell, moving on down

3. Type Electricity, then Enter.

4. Type Rent, then Enter.

5. Type VISA, then Enter, then Insurance, then Enter, then Cable TV, then Enter.

    Your selected range looks like figure 4.12 when you're done, unless you've missed something.

	A	B	C
1	Bills	Amount	Date Due
2	Telephone		
3	Electricity		
4	Rent	✛	
5	VISA		
6	Insurance		
7	Cable TV		
8			
9			
10			

Figure 4.12
After entering the names of the bills

The command key short-cut for saving in Excel is Command-S, just as it is in Word. Ditto for ClarisWorks.

How about saving what you've done?

I'll admit that this business of selecting a range takes a few seconds and that it really didn't do anything that Return wouldn't do by itself. You'll see how valuable the technique is as we enter the amounts and due dates.

Start by selecting the range from B2 to C7. You can do it the hard way, which involves a bit of mouse-dragging:

Click on B2 and drag to C7 (it works).

Or you can do it the all-time cool way (called, officially, *shift-clicking*):

1. Click on B2.

2. Hold the Shift key down and click on C7.

With either method you choose, the result should look like figure 4.13.

	A	B	C
1	Bills	Amount	Date Due
2	Telephone		
3	Electricity		
4	Rent		
5	VISA		
6	Insurance		
7	Cable TV		
8			
9			
10			

Figure 4.13
After selecting the range

The reason this second method is all-time cool is that it's so darned forgiving. Mousing, even with practice, isn't forgiving at all. Suppose you'd selected the wrong range (maybe you let go of the mouse too soon). Figure 4.14 shows one of the virtually unlimited ways to blow the selection.

	A	B	C	D
1	Bills	Amount	Date Due	
2	Telephone			
3	Electricity			
4	Rent			
5	VISA			
6	Insurance			
7	Cable TV			
8				

Figure 4.14
Blown selection (let go too soon)

How can shift-clicking save you now? Easily, that's how. Work along with me here:

1. Make the bad selection I made in figure 4.14.

2. Hold the Shift key and click on cell C7.

    Everything's perfect (figure 4.15).

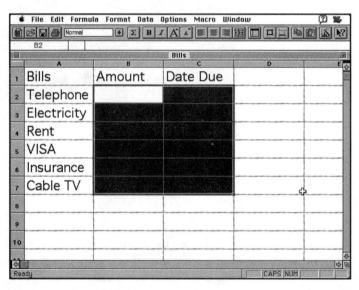

Figure 4.15
Perfect recovery via Shift-click technique

I'm not done with you yet. Suppose you change your mind now and want to select column D down to row 7 as well. No problem:

3. Hold the Shift key and click on cell D7.

It works. Practice shift-clicking until you're convinced it's cool, and until you're convinced you can do it when you want to.

4. Finish by being sure you've selected the proper range as shown in figure 4.15.

Now we're ready to enter the rest of our data.

1. Type any reasonable number. Press Enter (not Return).

Your number is entered into cell B2 and the active cell moves *right* to cell C2. Don't worry about the dollar sign; we'll do that automatically.

2. Type a date with slashes between the month, day, and year, for example, 9/1/93. Then press Enter.

The active cell jumps back to the Amount column, and down one row, ready for you to enter the next amount. Now you can see why this "select a range" idea is so handy: you can use the numeric keypad to type in the numbers, and the Enter key to enter them, and you can go through the entire range without using the mouse. It's a lot faster than clicking on each cell one by one via mouse.

I'll bet you can handle filling in the rest of the data on your own. Don't worry about the total; that comes next. Before you finish entering the data, though, try this little experiment (you've still got that range selected, right?):

1. Press the Enter key over and over and over. Hold it down.

Notice that the active cell is moving through the range, and that it *loops around back to the top* if you press Enter enough times. You can loop through the range as many times as you like.

2. Hold the Shift key down and press Enter.

The active cell moves backward, to the previous cell instead of the next cell.

This is very useful, especially if—by some freak of nature—you happen to make a mistake. Usually, you'll catch mistakes right after making them; with the Shift-Enter technique, you can simply go back, make the correction, and move on. This beats clicking on the cell you want to correct because Shift-Enter retains the

GENIUS TIP

Shift-clicking isn't restricted to spreadsheets. You can shift-click in word processing documents, in drawings—all over the place. The key: try it. You won't break anything by doing it wrong, so keep at it until you've got it down.

GENIUS TIP

Excel assumes that dates without years (10/31, for instance) refer to the current year. Thus, entering 10/31 and 10/31/93 give the same result, assuming that it's 1993 when you first enter the date. ClarisWorks does not make this assumption, so you always have to enter the year.

selection, while clicking with the mouse does not. Try it if you don't believe me.

By now, you've got a spreadsheet that looks something like the one shown in figure 4.16, but so far, your spreadsheet program's done nothing more than line up the rows and columns. Big deal. Now comes the impressive stuff: a *calculation.*

First, type the word Total in cell A9. Press the Tab key. (This is not the good part.)

> **n**
> **O** *Corrections are easy:*
> **t** *just get to the right*
> **E** *cell and type the*
> *correct data. Press*
> *Enter and you're done.*
> *No need to Delete or*
> *Backspace, just type*
> *what you want and*
> *move on.*

	File Edit Formula Format Data Options Macro Window		?

B2 | 122.56

Bills

	A	B	C	D	E
1	Bills	Amount	Date Due		
2	Telephone	122.56	9/1/93		
3	Electricity	14.62	9/3/93		
4	Rent	695	9/1/93		
5	VISA	321.21	8/28/93		
6	Insurance	245.36	8/19/93		
7	Cable TV	11.95	9/15/93		
8					
9					
10					

Ready   CAPS NUM

Figure 4.16
The spreadsheet so far

GENIUS TIP

Every Excel calculation and every ClarisWorks calculation begins with an equals sign.

Follow these next steps carefully:

1. Assuming that B9 is the active cell, press the equals key (the one on the keypad is easier to find, but the one next to Delete is fine, too).

2. Click on cell B2.

3. Press the plus sign. (I'd advise using the one on the keypad, to avoid pressing Delete or = by mistake.)

4. Click on cell B3. Press the plus sign.

5. Click on cell B4. Press the plus sign.

n
o
t
E
As you're doing this typing and clicking, you're building a formula. The formula is displayed in the formula bar in almost every spreadsheet program (some display the formula in the cells themselves, but this is not the norm). ClarisWorks calls the formula bar the entry bar. Look near the top of any spreadsheet window and you'll find the formula or entry bar.

And so on and so on and so on, until you've finally clicked on cell B7. *Do not type a plus sign after clicking on cell B7.* The formula bar should look like the one shown in figure 4.17.

Figure 4.17
The formula, in the formula bar

6. Press Enter.

Wow! You've entered a formula, and it works.

Quick: hit Command-S and save the thing.

On the off chance that something went wrong, here's what it probably was (and how to fix it):

- You've got a plus sign at the end of the formula. Solve this one by deleting that last plus.

- Everything seems OK except the total looks like "######." The number signs tell you that the column isn't wide enough to show the total. Solve this problem by dragging the top of the vertical bar separating column B from column C, found between the "B" box and the "C" box, to the right.

Here's an easier way to add up the amounts:

1. Click on cell B9. Press Delete to clear the existing formula, then press Enter to show the program that you mean it.

   The formula is gone. Make sure cell B9 is still active (just click on it if it isn't).

2. Type the equals sign, as before.

3. Click on cell B2, as before, but this time, do NOT type a plus sign.

4. Click on cell B3.

   Guess what? Your spreadsheet assumes you want to add things, so it enters a plus sign for you.

5. Click on B4, then B5, then B6, then B7. Press Enter.

   Hey wow!

It happens that there are other ways to add up those bills. Some of them are quite handy:

- In Excel, click in cell B9, then double-click the AutoSum tool (figure 4.18). Excel interprets your actions to mean: "Add up everything above cell B9 and put the answer into B9."

Figure 4.18
Excel's AutoSum tool

If you're using Excel 4.0 and don't see a toolbar, you're going to have a hard time finding the AutoSum tool. Display the Standard toolbar by choosing **Toolbars...** from the **Options** menu, clicking on "Standard" in the resulting dialog box (figure 4.19), and then clicking on the Show button.

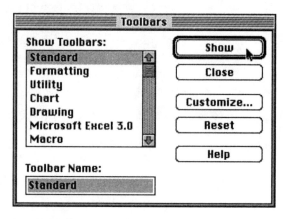

Figure 4.19
Toolbars dialog box (Excel 4.0 only)

- In ClarisWorks, click on cell B2 and shift-click on cell B9. Then press the Auto-Sum tool in the Shortcuts palette (figure 4.20). This is about as different from Excel as you can get, which is odd since the tools have almost the same names and icons. ClarisWorks translates your actions like this: "If the selected range (B2 to B9) ends with a blank cell, add everything above that blank last cell (B9) and put the answer into that blank last cell (B9)."

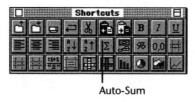

Auto-Sum

Figure 4.20
ClarisWorks' Auto-Sum tool

If you're using ClarisWorks and don't see a Shortcuts palette, choose **Shortcuts** from the **File** menu and **Show Shortcuts** from the pop-out submenu (figure 4.21).

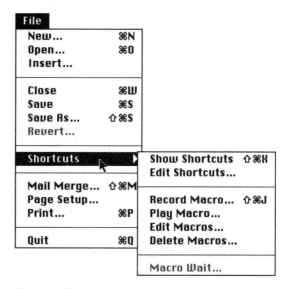

Figure 4.21
Showing Shortcuts (in ClarisWorks)

Just for fun, change the amount of one of the bills. Press Enter. *The total changed.* That's what's *supposed* to happen. Pretty neat.

I mentioned before that spreadsheet programs are good at math. Figure 4.22 shows Excel's Paste Function dialog box, available via the **Formula** menu. The spreadsheet module in ClarisWorks has a similar list of functions, under the **Edit** menu (figure 4.23). Scroll through the functions in the Paste Function list; someday it'll help you to know that a spreadsheet program can figure out car payments, averages, sines and cosines, and other complicated calculations. Best place to learn about these functions? The manuals, or, if you can wait, a future book by me.

■■■■■■■■■■■■■■■■■■■■■■■■■■■■■■■■■■■■■■

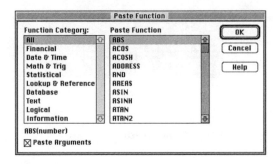

Figure 4.22
Excel 4.0's Paste Function dialog box

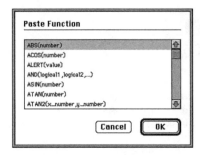

Figure 4.23
ClarisWorks 2.0's Paste Function dialog box

Formatting

The spreadsheet is now functional, but it's ugly. Let's fix it up so it looks like the one shown in figure 4.24.

Like everything else on a Mac, formatting a spreadsheet follows the "first select something, then do something to it" rule. Let's start by formatting the column headings so they're bold.

1. Click on cell A1.

2. Shift-click on cell C1.

   Your selection should look like the one shown in figure 4.25.

3. Click on the "B" (for Bold) button in the Standard toolbar (Excel) or the Shortcuts palette (ClarisWorks).

   Figure 4.26 shows you what you're looking for.

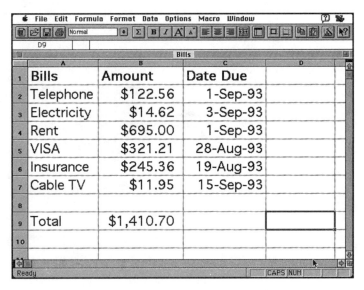

Figure 4.24
Formatted spreadsheet

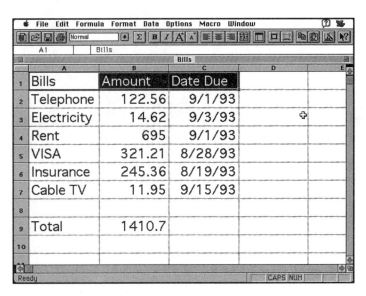

Figure 4.25
Column headings, selected

Bold Button ─────────────

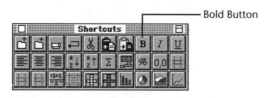

Bold Button ──────

Figure 4.26
Bold buttons for Excel and ClarisWorks

How about a little Command-S action? It's always good to Save.

The spreadsheet's coming along, except that the amounts need dollar signs and the dates don't look like dates. We'll put dollar signs on the amounts first; this is called *applying a number format*.

1. Select the cells you want to format (B2 through B9).

2. Click and hold down the arrow in the Standard toolbar to the right of the word "Normal." Figure 4.27 shows you the place to be.

Click here ──────

n *If you want to do*
o *things the hard way,*
t *try choosing Number*
E *from the Format menu.*
You get more choices,
but the process is much
more complicated.

Figure 4.27
The right place to click

With the mouse button down, you can see the list of predefined number formats that Excel provides. Many others exist (choose **Number...** from the **Format** menu and you'll see what I mean), but the ones in the Standard toolbar are often all you need.

3. Drag down to Currency and let go.

Your numbers now have dollar signs and two decimal places (figure 4.28). You may need to make the columns wider after performing this move; if so, just grab the bar between the headings for column B and column C and drag it to the right.

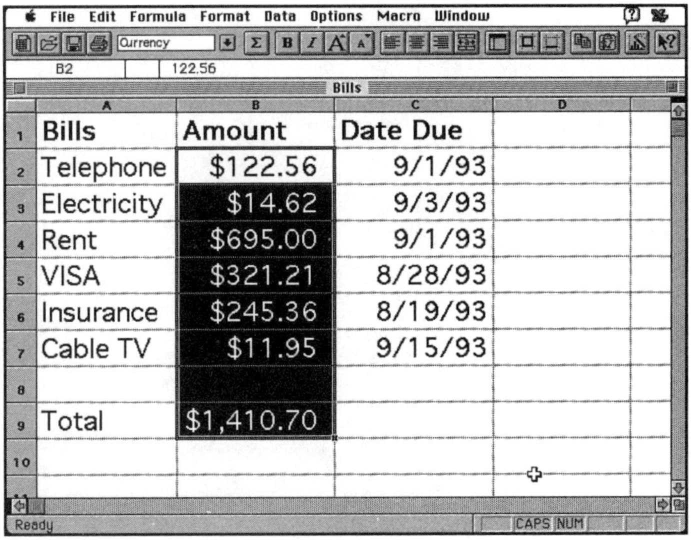

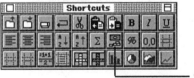

Figure 4.28
After formatting as Currency

It's always better to do things this way (enter plain numbers and let Excel do the formatting) than it is to enter the dollar signs yourself. It's easier on you (less to type) and it's better for the program.

In ClarisWorks, click on the Currency Format button in the Shortcuts palette (figure 4.29).

Currency Button

Figure 4.29
Currency Format button (ClarisWorks)

All that's left is that column of dates. Looks bad now, but we'll fix it up pronto.

1. Select the dates (from C2 through C7).

   Sorry to say that there's nothing in the toolbar for us this time. We're going to have to go into the **Format** menu. It won't hurt, but it's not pretty either. Don't wander off—you may have trouble finding your way out.

2. Choose **Number...** from the **Format** menu (figure 4.30). You'll get the dialog box shown in figure 4.31 if you're using Excel, or the one shown in figure 4.32 if you're using ClarisWorks.

Figure 4.30
Choosing Number... from the Format menu

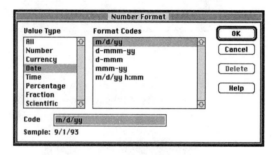

Figure 4.31
Number Format dialog box (Excel 4.0)

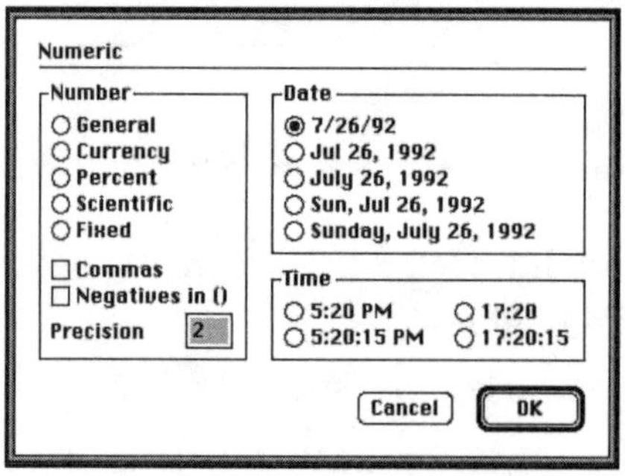

Figure 4.32
Number Format dialog box (ClarisWorks 2.0)

3. Choose a date format by clicking on one.

4. Click on OK.

   You're done.

Depending on the format you chose, your spreadsheet looks more or less like figure 4.33. You might need to make the columns wider to display the newly formatted dates. If so, just drag the bar separating the headings for column C and column D to the right. Don't forget to save.

	Bills	Amount	Date Due	
1	Bills	Amount	Date Due	
2	Telephone	$122.56	1-Sep-93	
3	Electricity	$14.62	3-Sep-93	
4	Rent	$695.00	1-Sep-93	
5	VISA	$321.21	28-Aug-93	
6	Insurance	$245.36	19-Aug-93	
7	Cable TV	$11.95	15-Sep-93	
8				
9	Total	$1,410.70		
10				

Figure 4.33
The finished spreadsheet

GENIUS TIP

A truly great way to recover from a truly bad move is to quit without saving. If, for example, you accidentally erased the formula that

continues

Let's quit. Have a cup of coffee. (Is anyone out there counting?) We'll come back in a minute to do some cutting, copying, and pasting. Then we'll make a chart.

1. Choose **Quit** from the **File** menu (this should be old hat by now).

2. If you're asked to save changes, think about it, then answer appropriately.

3. See if you can find your spreadsheet. It ought to be in the same folder as your spreadsheet program. Look there. It'll look something like figure 4.34.

Bills

Figure 4.34
Excel spreadsheet icon

continued

totaled up the bills, you'd probably wish you hadn't. If it was too late for Undo (perhaps you'd made another move since), the only way out would be to quit and say "no" when asked to save changes. I do it all the time. Nothing to be ashamed of.

GENIUS TIP

The Modified Boyce Method for selecting cells via the keyboard is very popular among Those In The Know. Try it:

    1. Use cursor keys to move to cell A9.

    2. Hold the Shift key down, and while it's down, tap the right arrow key. This selects cell B9. (You can continue to hold the Shift key and tap arrow keys as long as you like.)

Most people feel more in control of the selection process when using this technique.

Cutting, Copying, and Pasting (and a Surprise Bonus)

Back so soon?

Almost done, gang. Hang in there. You still need to know how to move stuff around, how to print, and how to make charts. Here we go!

1. Locate the icon for the Bills spreadsheet you made earlier.

2. Double-click on the icon.
   The Bills spreadsheet opens.

Let's try moving the Total calculation and the Total label down one row. It's a matter of selecting the right cells, cutting them, and pasting them somewhere else.

1. Select cells A9 and B9 (use any method you want, but you'll be on my good side if you choose the Modified Boyce Method).

2. Choose **Cut** from the **Edit** menu (figure 4.35).

3. Select cells A10 and B10, any way you want to.

4. Choose **Paste** from the **Edit** menu (figure 4.36).

   Whaddya know—it worked! (And the formula still adds up.)

I'll bet you're not so impressed with that last genius tip. You will be. See, there are only two ways to make cut and paste work. One way is the way you did it in the example: select cells to cut from, and cut; then select cells to paste to, and paste. This method fails when the *paste to* range isn't exactly the same size and shape as the *cut from* range. So, had you accidentally selected three cells in Step 3 above, the paste wouldn't have worked, and you'd have seen the dreaded different shapes dialog box, shown in figure 4.37.

Figure 4.35
Choosing Cut from the Edit menu

Figure 4.36
Choosing Paste from the Edit menu

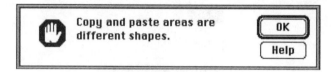

Figure 4.37
The dreaded different shapes dialog box

You worked a little bit harder in Step 3 than you needed to. In fact, all you really had to do was click on cell A10 (to show where you wanted to start pasting), and everything would have worked just fine.

I said there were two ways to make the cut and paste work, and here's the second (the genius) way: select cells to cut from, and cut; then select a *single* cell (where you want the pasting to start), and paste. This always works. Always. If you're cutting and pasting large ranges of cells you'll find it *much* easier to select the starting cell for pasting rather than selecting a range that exactly matches the shape of the cells that you cut. I *always* use the "starting point" method. You will, too, once you've seen the different shapes dialog a couple of hundred times. Your Uncle Christian is looking out for you.

If you're using Excel 4.0, there's an even better way to move cells around. It's called *drag and drop* and it's just plain perfect. Dig this:

1. Select some cells. How about the entire spreadsheet, from A1 to C10?

   Your screen should look like figure 4.38.

If there is something in the cells you are pasting to, it will be replaced by what-ever you are pasting. So be careful and remember Undo.

	A	B	C	D
1	Bills	Amount	Date Due	
2	Telephone	$122.56	1-Sep-93	
3	Electricity	$14.62	3-Sep-93	
4	Rent	$695.00	1-Sep-93	
5	VISA	$321.21	28-Aug-93	
6	Insurance	$245.36	19-Aug-93	
7	Cable TV	$11.95	15-Sep-93	
8				
9				
10	Total	$1,410.70		

Figure 4.38
After selecting everything

2. Carefully, slowly, move the cursor toward any edge of the selected range. Your cursor will change from a cross (figure 4.39) to a pointer (figure 4.40). When this happens, stop. You're in the right place.

Figure 4.39
The standard Excel cursor

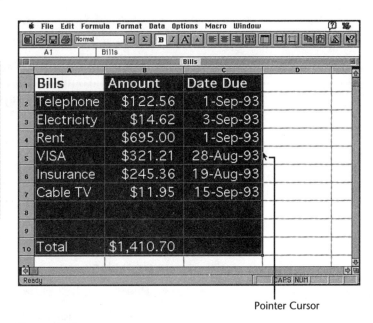

Pointer Cursor

Figure 4.40
When you're in the right spot

3. Click, with the pointer, on the edge of the selected range and drag it to any location. Let go.

   The whole selection moves, and the calculation still works. It's amazing.

   (If you drag the selected range into cells that are narrower than what you're dragging you may see the "#####" problem we ran into earlier. As before, make the column wide enough by dragging the vertical line between column labels and watch your "#####" problem disappear.)

That's it. Dragging and dropping doesn't work in ClarisWorks, but that's the way it goes. (It does, however, work in Microsoft Word 5 and 5.1; poke around in the Preferences area and turn on the drag and drop option.)

Let's print.

Printing

I suppose, after making this incredible spreadsheet, you'll want copies for everyone you know. So much for the paperless office.

There are two ways to print an Excel spreadsheet: the easy-but-dumb way, and the only-slightly-harder-but-oh-so-much-cooler way. I'll show you both. I trust you to make the right decision.

(There's just one way to print a ClarisWorks spreadsheet, which makes the decision easier.)

The Easy-But-Dumb Way to Print an Excel Spreadsheet

Here it is, in all its glory:

1. Choose **Print...** from the **File** menu.

2. Click on the Print button in the dialog box (figure 4.41).

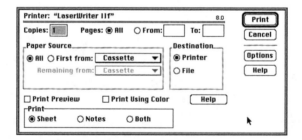

Figure 4.41
Excel's Print dialog box

This is the dumb way to print, because you're stuck with all of Excel's default settings. If you choose this easy method, you'll get your spreadsheet alright, but you'll also see a ridiculous

"Page 1" on the bottom (as if there's a need to number a one-page spreadsheet) and a "Bills" across the top (which could be good, but not the way the Excel default handles it). You also get row and column headings, and a grid pattern, which may louse up the look of your document. All in all, you get your stuff, but it looks cheap. Try it anyway (sigh).

Printing a ClarisWorks spreadsheet is similar, but you do get control over gridlines and row and column headings after choosing **Print...** (figure 4.42).

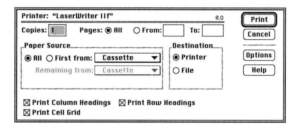

Figure 4.42
Print dialog box for the ClarisWorks spreadsheet module

Only-Slightly-Harder-But-Oh-So-Much-Cooler Way to Print an Excel Spreadsheet

Here's the right way to print an Excel spreadsheet (or an Excel chart, for that matter):

Choose **Print Preview** from the **File** menu (figure 4.43). This simple choice, physically only fractions of an inch above **Print...** but worlds apart in terms of worthiness, transforms your screen into the one shown in figure 4.44.

This is a powerful place to be. For starters, you now know how your printed page will look. You can zoom out (that's what the Zoom button's for) to see the whole page, and you can zoom back to see the words and numbers.

You can change margins (that's what the Margins button is for): click on the button, then drag the square black handles around (figure 4.45). You can change column widths this way, too.

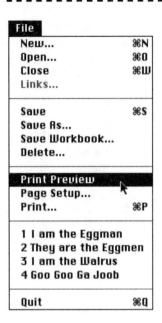

Figure 4.43
Choosing **Print Preview** from the **File** menu

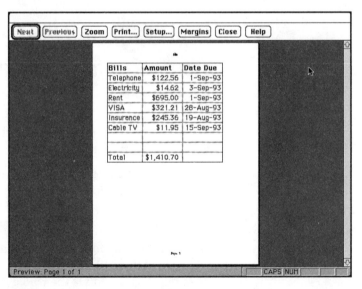

Figure 4.44
After choosing **Print Preview**

You can open the Page Setup dialog box by clicking the Setup button; figure 4.46 shows the plethora of options you'll find. When you've finally got it right, you can click on the Print button and you're off to the races.

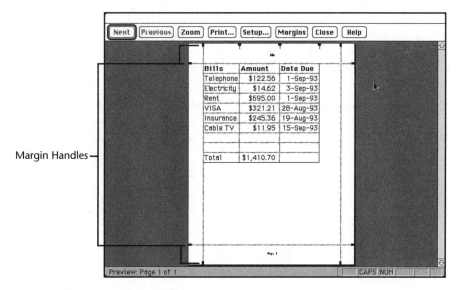

Margin Handles

Figure 4.45
Margin handles

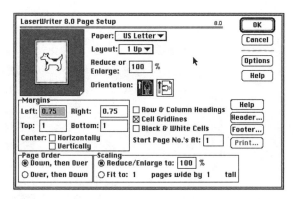

Figure 4.46
Page Setup dialog box

In case you absent-mindedly choose **Print...** instead of **Print Preview**, click on the Print Preview checkbox (figure 4.47) and then click on the Print button. This takes you to the same Print Preview screen you would have been at had you chosen it directly. Yes, it's a confusing world, but that's Excel for you.

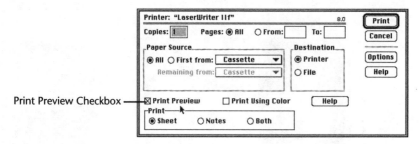

Print Preview Checkbox ——

Figure 4.47
Print Preview checkbox

Now, as advertised, your mini-mini charting lesson.

Charting

What would you rather look at: numbers (figure 4.48) or pictures (figure 4.49)? Both represent the same information, but pictures are easier to grasp.

Bills	Amount	Date Due	
Telephone	$122.56	1-Sep-93	
Electricity	$14.62	3-Sep-93	
Rent	$695.00	1-Sep-93	
VISA	$321.21	28-Aug-93	
Insurance	$245.36	19-Aug-93	
Cable TV	$11.95	15-Sep-93	
Total	$1,410.70		

Figure 4.48
Numbers

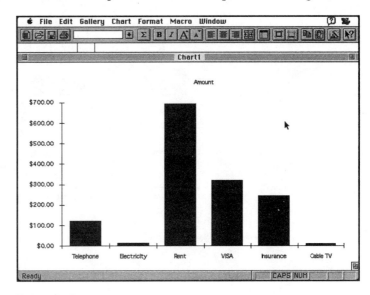

Figure 4.49
Pictures

Excel and ClarisWorks let you turn numbers into charts without working hard at all. We'll do it in four steps with Excel:

1. Select the range of cells to chart (figure 4.50). Make your range look like mine (select just the names of the bills and the amounts).

	A	B
1	Bills	Amount
2	Telephone	$122.56
3	Electricity	$14.62
4	Rent	$695.00
5	VISA	$321.21
6	Insurance	$245.36
7	Cable TV	$11.95

Figure 4.50
Select these cells

2. Choose **New** from the **File** menu.

You'll get a dialog box like the one shown in figure 4.51.

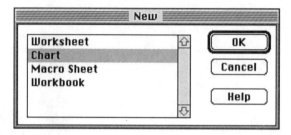

Figure 4.51
New dialog box

3. You want a chart, so click on Chart.

4. Click on OK.

You're done. You should see something like the chart shown in figure 4.52 on your screen.

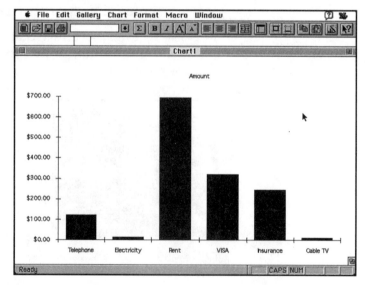

Figure 4.52
Your first chart

That was easy, right? If you're using ClarisWorks, it's even easier: would you believe *three* steps? Check it out:

1. Select the range of cells to chart. Make it look like figure 4.50 (just the names of the bills and the amounts).

2. Choose **Shortcuts** from the **File** menu and **Show Short-cuts** from the pop-out submenu (of course, this may already be showing; if so, don't worry about doing it again).

3. Click on the Bar Chart button in the Shortcuts palette (figure 4.53).

Unbelievable!

— Bar Chart Button

Figure 4.53
Bar Chart button in ClarisWorks' Shortcuts palette

Here's the cool part (as if charts weren't cool enough already): whether you used Excel or ClarisWorks, your chart and your spreadsheet are connected. That means that when your spreadsheet changes, your chart changes, too. In Excel, rearrange the windows so you can see both on your screen, as shown in figure 4.54 (I know you can do this: resize the windows with the grow box, and drag the windows by their title bars.) In ClarisWorks, just drag the chart off to the side so you can see the spreadsheet numbers.

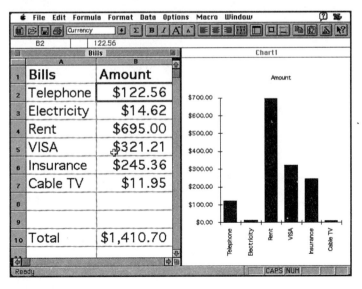

Figure 4.54
Chart and spreadsheet showing (Excel)

Now make a change (in the spreadsheet) to the amount of a bill. Press Enter while keeping an eye on the chart. The chart changes. This sent a chill down my spine the first time I saw it—you talk about *power*. Very, very cool.

Now a word (or maybe two) about saving the fabulous chart you just made. The chart and the spreadsheet in Excel are saved separately. If, in Excel, you really want to save the chart and the spreadsheet as a single document, grab that li'l ol' Excel manual and look the rascal up (try *Excel User's Guide 1*). (Hey, sorry to send you elsewhere, but this *is* a basics books after all!)

GENIUS TIP

You can make a lot more than bar/column charts. Poke around a little and you'll find out how. Here are some hints from your ol' Uncle Christian: in Excel, look for the Gallery menu; in ClarisWorks, choose Modify Chart from the menu.

The chart and the spreadsheet in ClarisWorks are already saved as a single document.

Time for coffee. And a quiz.

1. Can you find your spreadsheet program?

2. Can you move around in a spreadsheet?

3. Can you enter data where you want to enter it?

4. Can you enter a formula?

5. Can you format text?

6. Can you format numbers?

7. Can you make columns wider?

8. Can you cut and paste cells?

9. Can you make a chart?

10. Can you print stuff out?

11. Would you like to dance?

Chapter 5
Software Smørgasbörd

This is where the fun begins. The first four chapters were like eating your vegetables. The next three are like dessert. The last two are like burping.

Chapters 5, 6, and 7 are full of good stuff and there's something for everyone. This chapter, the Software Smørgasbörd, introduces you to three classes of everyday business software: art programs, page layout programs, and database management programs, plus a special group of exceptional software that I personally dig. You'll see what these programs do, learn what your choices are, and find out how to use the rascals to do the things you want. I'll also tell you which programs I think are the best in each category (I crown 'em King).

Art Programs

Art programs fall neatly into three groups: drawing programs, painting programs, and programs that are both. Drawing programs are superficially similar to painting programs; you'll shortly see, however, that each type of program has shortcomings the other type doesn't. We'll cover drawing programs first.

Drawing Programs

The King: Canvas 3.0

Pretenders to the Throne: MacDraw Pro, SuperPaint, drawing module from ClarisWorks

Drawing programs (also called *draw programs*) are just what you need to create floor plans, diagrams, and organization charts. If the picture you want is mostly straight lines and smooth curves, use a drawing program. Figure 5.1 shows a drawing created with a drawing program.

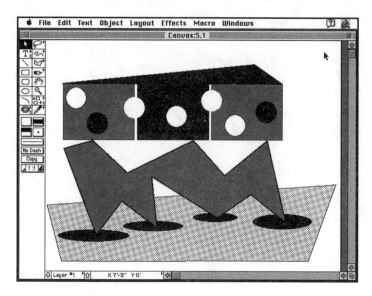

Figure 5.1
A sample drawing

The very first Macintosh drawing program, MacDraw, introduced tools and techniques that are still being used. In fact,
you'll see elements of drawing programs in some word processors, database management programs, and page layout programs. Probably other places, too. Keep your eyes open.

The best way to learn about this kind of program is to use one.
Allow me to demonstrate.

Figure 5.2 shows a generic draw program tool palette. Select a
tool from the palette by clicking on it. Once you've clicked on it,
move your cursor into the document and use the tool.

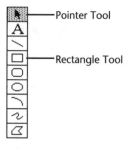

Figure 5.2
Generic draw program tool palette

n o t e   *This will work best if you get out your trusty draw program and follow along. Look for the software titles I mentioned earlier or for any applications with the word "draw" in the title. When you find one, open it up and follow along. Even if you're using a different program than I am, it will still work similarly.*

Most of the tools are ridiculously easy to use. Take, for example, the rectangle tool:

1. Click on the rectangle tool.

2. Click in the drawing and hold the mouse button down.

3. Drag down and to the right until the rectangle's the right size, then let go.

You get something looking like figure 5.3.

Figure 5.3
A rectangle

The neat thing about drawing programs is that they let you make adjustments to the things you've drawn. It's easy to change this hollow rectangle to one that's filled with gray by clicking on a fill pattern palette (figure 5.4); the rectangle now looks like figure 5.5.

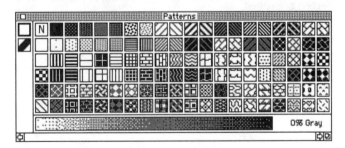

Figure 5.4
A fill pattern palette

GENIUS TIP

Want to draw a square or a perfect circle? Hold the Shift key down while you drag.

Figure 5.5
Gray rectangle

It's also very easy to duplicate the rectangle. Select the rectangle (you can tell when an item is selected because square black knobs appear at the corners). When it's selected, look for a **Duplicate** command in the **Edit** menu. You'll get a second, identical rectangle after you select **Duplicate**. Figure 5.6 shows how the duplicate looks.

mAC LiNGO

The square black knobs that appear when something is selected are called "handles."

Figure 5.6
Two identical rectangles

(In case you've been napping, wake yourself up, because the stuff I'm about to tell you is very important. Blow this and you'll be doomed.)

Suppose you wanted to rearrange the rectangles, make one smaller, and color the smaller one black. There's nothing to it. The first thing to do is select the rectangle you want to work on—that is, tell your drawing program which rectangle you want to change to black. *You do this by clicking the desired rectangle with the pointer tool.*

GENIUS TIP

You also could have duplicated the rectangle by using good ol' copy and paste. Here's how you do it. First, select the rectangle by clicking on it. Next, choose Copy from the File menu (come on, you're a pro, just use Command-C). Last, choose Paste (I hope you used Command-V). There you have it, another rectangle. Ta-da!

Now that you've selected the proper rectangle, click on the solid black pattern in the fill pattern palette. Presto: the rectangle changes to black (figure 5.7). *Notice that the other rectangle remains unchanged.* It's sort of like selecting text, then making it bold: the only stuff that changes is the stuff you have selected.

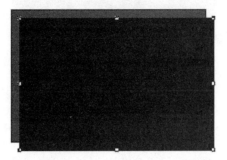

Figure 5.7
After changing a rectangle's fill to solid black

Want to resize the black rectangle? No problem. Be sure you've got the pointer tool and not some other tool, then click on a handle (figure 5.8) and drag the corner anywhere you want. The rectangle redraws itself when you let go (figure 5.9).

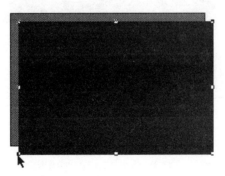

Figure 5.8
Clicking on a handle

You may not have realized it, but the fact that the rectangle redraws itself when you move one of its corners is pretty darned amazing. Technically speaking, the rectangle knows that it's a rectangle, and that it has to have four straight sides connected by 90 degree angles. It also knows that you've assigned it a fill pattern (and optionally a fill color, a line thickness, and a line color). In short, the rectangle is an "object" and it always remembers that fact. (Everything else you create in a drawing program is an object too, with its own attributes and characteristics.) Drawing programs are quite different from painting programs in this respect—different enough that drawing programs are sometimes called "object-oriented" art programs.

Figure 5.9
The resized rectangle

Moving an object (in this case, a rectangle) is easy as pie: Either click on the object itself (not on a handle) and drag, or select the object and use the cursor keys. Dragging is usually easier, except when you need to move something a tiny little bit. That's the time to use cursor keys. Figure 5.10 shows our little black rectangle, moved up and to the right.

Figure 5.10
Rectangles, after moving the little one

Now, suppose we want to put the big rectangle in front of the little one. Nothing to it: just click on the big rectangle (use the pointer tool) and search the menus for something called **Move to Front** or **Send to Front** or anything similar. Figure 5.11 shows how it looks when you do it right, and in case you weren't paying attention, this was a darned neat move.

Figure 5.11
Big rectangle in the front

The neat thing about that last move is you can shuffle objects forward and backward endlessly. You don't have to draw your objects in any particular order because you can always rearrange them later. Drawings you make will be a combination of primitive shapes (rectangles, ovals, and lines) and text boxes, each of which you create individually. Then you assemble and arrange these objects into your finished masterpiece (Picasso would be so proud). Figure 5.12 shows such a document (notice how virtually any regular shape can be created with clever stacking of these primitive objects).

Figure 5.12
Nothing but rectangles, ovals, and lines

When it comes to excellent printed output, there's nothing like a draw program. Each line, each curve, each pattern comes out better on the paper than it does on the screen (and they don't look bad on the screen). This is due to the object-oriented nature of drawing programs, and it turns out to be good news and bad news.

The good news is everything you draw comes out gorgeous. The bad news is, it's tough to draw some things. For example, draw something with soft edges, like a cloud, or something with an irregular fill pattern, like a tree. You can make some interesting attempts (figure 5.13), but even if you get it right, you'll have worked too hard. This is a weakness of drawing programs: they're no good at drawing natural-looking scenes.

Figure 5.13
Some interesting attempts

It just so happens that painting programs, which aren't good at producing smooth curves and straight lines, are quite good at producing natural-looking pictures. Funny how this works out.

Painting Programs

The King: SuperPaint

Pretenders to the Throne: MacPaint, UltraPaint, painting module in ClarisWorks

Look at figure 5.14, created with a painting program. Notice the texture and the natural look, especially compared to the figures in the drawing section. You can't make pictures like figure 5.14 in a drawing program—you *must* use a paint program.

Painting programs are sometimes called "bitmap" art programs. That means that the pictures you make with painting programs are collections (maps) of dots (bits), rather like mosaics. The essence of painted pictures is therefore completely different than that of drawn pictures, which are collections of *objects*.

Figure 5.14
A painted picture

The "dotty" nature of paint programs is both a blessing and a curse. The blessing part is simple to understand: you can edit an individual dot on the screen, changing its color to anything you want it to be, regardless of the color of the surrounding dots. You also get to use tools like spray paint cans and paint brushes to obtain natural, irregular effects (figure 5.15) without trying hard at all.

Figure 5.15
Spray paint and paint brush effects

The curse of the dots is that there's no intelligence to a painting. You can paint a rectangle and (using the Paint Bucket) fill it with gray, and you can paint a smaller black rectangle on top of it (figure 5.16), but those rectangles don't remember that they're rectangles with fill, size, and line attributes. They don't even remember that they're separate objects (which makes sense, since they're not objects at all). When you resize a painted rectangle, the fill pattern gets yucky (figure 5.17), and when you try to shuffle the order of painted rectangles, you can't—there's no **Move to Front** command—and besides, the two rectangles are really just one big blob of dots, completely melded into one. You can no more remove one of the rectangles from the painting in figure 5.16 than you can remove the sugar from a glass of Kool-Aid. It's part of the mix.

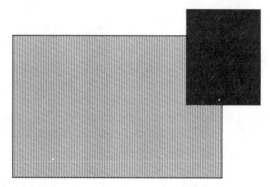

Figure 5.16
Two painted rectangles

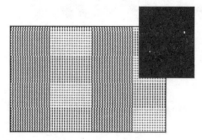

Figure 5.17
Yucky fill pattern after resizing

Figure 5.18 shows the typical painting tools; you'll notice that there's no pointer. Instead, there's a Selection Rectangle and a Lasso.

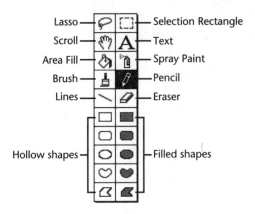

Figure 5.18
Typical painting tools

The Selection Rectangle is easy to use: just click and drag across the region you wish to select. When you do so, you'll see a flashing dashed outline showing you what you selected. If you click anywhere within the dashed outline (figure 5.19) you'll be able to drag the selected area anywhere you want (figure 5.20). Notice that the white space, which you probably thought of as "nothing" and not as *white* space, is also selected and therefore also moved.

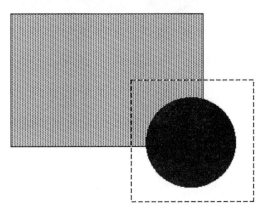

Figure 5.19
Selected area (dashed outline)

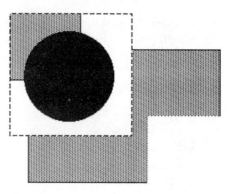

Figure 5.20
After dragging an area selected with the Selection Rectangle

The Lasso is different in two ways. First, your selection can be
any shape: regular, irregular, you name it. Second, the Lasso
tightens up when you let go of the mouse button, stopping only
when it hits a non-white screen dot. When you move the
lassoed area (by clicking on it and dragging), you'll notice that
the white space doesn't come along (figure 5.21). This is generally good.

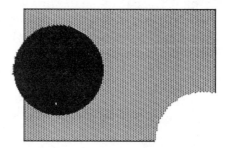

Figure 5.21
After dragging an area selected with the Lasso

*A screen dot is sometimes
called a "pixel", which is a
shortened form of the term
"Picture Element." Who
thinks of these things,
anyway?*

It's important to notice that, regardless of your selection tool,
you'll always leave a hole in your painting (figure 5.22), and
sometimes that's not what you want. This doesn't happen in
the draw programs.

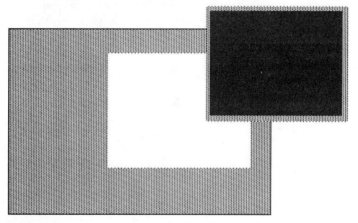

Figure 5.22
Leaving a hole

Draw and Paint Combination Programs

The King: Canvas and SuperPaint (tie)

Pretenders to the throne: Draw and Paint modules in ClarisWorks 2.0

Once upon a time drawing programs were drawing programs and painting programs were painting programs. Drawing programs were used for drawing pictures full of straight lines and smooth curves, and painting programs were used for painting artsy stuff (basically everything else). Then someone had the brilliant idea of combining the two types of programs into one, with one *layer* for the painting and another layer for the drawing. This program, SuperPaint, spawned a bunch of imitators, because the combined approach really was a heck of a good idea.

SuperPaint is better at painting than it is at drawing. Canvas is better at drawing than it is at painting. (That's why there's a tie for the position of King of the Combo Art programs.) Regardless of which you use, you'll find the combination programs to be just the ticket. You can draw regular objects in the drawing layer (and resize, and fill, and color those objects all you want), and do special artsy effects in the paint layer. For example, the draw layer is good for text (figure 5.23) while text in the paint layer can be less than great (figure 5.24). The cool thing is you can see both layers at once, so when you print you get the benefits of both. Figure 5.25 shows a picture made with Canvas, partly using draw tools and partly using paint tools.

Far out, man

Secret message

Figure 5.23
Text created and manipulated in the draw layer

Scruff City

Hi, Mom

Figure 5.24
Text created and manipulated in the paint layer

GENIUS TIP

This is the best tip in the book. Ready?

When working with text, always use the draw layer. When you do, you get smooth text, no matter what you do to it (figure 5.23 shows some examples). Text created in the painting layer looks OK on the screen when entered, but looks (and prints) lousy once you do anything to it (figure 5.24). Besides, painted text can't be edited.

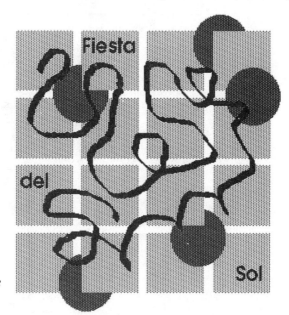

Figure 5.25
Made with a combo program

Between you and me, my favorite combo art program is Canvas, by virtue of being clearly the best drawing program on the Mac while including more than decent painting tools.

That's it for art programs. On to the page layout category.

n *Other programs,*
o *notably Aldus*
t *FreeHand and Adobe*
E *Illustrator, are excellent tools but not for beginners. You'll notice, though, if you ever do try them, that their tool palettes are a lot like those for the drawing programs we've talked about.*

Page Layout Programs

The King: PageMaker

Pretenders to the throne: QuarkXPress, ReadySetGo!

Page layout programs enable you to create books, magazines, and advertisements from elements created elsewhere. (You generally don't create documents from scratch in page layout programs because each element is better created with a specialized program.) The typical page layout document contains text typed with a word processing program and pictures created in an art program. Figure 5.26 shows such a document, assembled in PageMaker using words from Microsoft Word and pictures from Canvas.

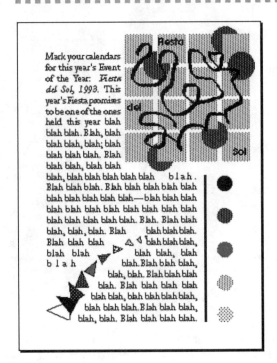

Figure 5.26
PageMaker document

PageMaker was the first page layout program and had a substantial headstart on the rest. Although the rest have caught up to PageMaker in terms of capabilities (in some cases surpassed it), none is as nice to use. That's why PageMaker is Boyce's choice for page layout work.

Figure 5.27 shows the PageMaker toolbox. Recognize anything? Sure you do. The Pointer's the same Pointer as in the drawing programs. And there's the same Rectangle tool and the same Line tool and the same Oval tool. Plus, there's the same Rounded-Corner Rectangle tool. The only tools you don't know about are the Perpendicular Line tool (for drawing vertical and horizontal lines without struggling) and the Cropping tool (for cropping pictures down to what you want).

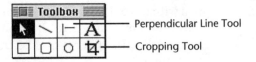

Perpendicular Line Tool

Cropping Tool

Figure 5.27
PageMaker toolbox

MAC LINGO

The tools have different names, depending on who you ask. PageMaker calls the Rectangle tool the "Square-Corner" tool. As if there are other kinds of corners.

Why would you use a page layout program rather than a drawing program? Why not lay out your pages in an all-in-one program like ClarisWorks, or a feature-heavy word processor like MacWrite Pro or Word? That's an excellent question.

The first reason to use a page layout program is *control*. PageMaker (and its harder to use arch-rival, QuarkXPress) give you unbelievable control, especially over text. Line spacing, word spacing, spacing between letters, and even the width of individual characters are yours to control, all to unbelievable degrees.

The second reason to use a page layout program is *capability* Page layout programs are ready, willing, and able to handle long (100 pages-plus) documents. Most word processors aren't. Page layout programs are able to give you different headers and footers (the stuff that's printed across the tops and bottoms of the pages, like page numbers and chapter titles) on different kinds of pages. Most word processors aren't. And they're able to import just about any kind of text and any kind of graphic, no matter where it came from. Most word processors can't, or won't.

The third reason to use a page layout program is that your stuff just looks better coming out. I use ClarisWorks for everyday stuff and PageMaker for stuff that matters. I'd use PageMaker for everything, but it would be like swatting flies with a bazooka. Definitely overkill. Besides, PageMaker files are on the large side: Large PageMaker documents take up twice as much storage space as large ClarisWorks documents, and small ones take up *four* times as much. That's a waste of space for everyday documents.

So far, our smørgasbörd is heavy on art, light on everything else. That'll change, starting now, as I introduce *database management* programs.

Database Management Programs

The King: FileMaker Pro

Pretenders to the Throne: all the others. Nothing else is close.

Database management programs are programs that manage databases. (I had to say that. Sorry.) The database might store

information about customers, invoices, party guests, police beatings—you name it. (Figures 5.28 and 5.29 show some other examples.) The database management program helps you find the data you want and presents it in the way you want. If you're looking to keep track of stuff, a database management program is the way to do it, and FileMaker Pro is the one to buy. Definitely Boyce's choice.

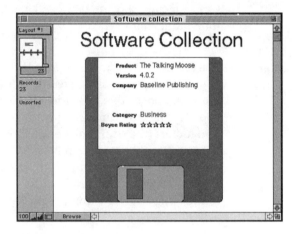

Figure 5.28
Software collection

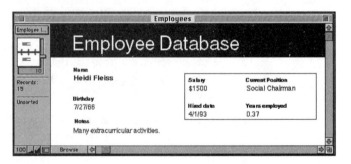

Figure 5.29
Employees

FileMaker, out of the box, doesn't know beans about what you want to keep track of. It's like a word processor: totally blank, ready for you to get to work. You get to work by telling FileMaker what things you want to keep track of; you do this by defining *fields*.

Defining fields is a simple matter of deciding what kind of information you're keeping track of and how you want to break

it up. Once you've told FileMaker what the fields will be, you're given a form, containing the fields, and that's where you enter the data. Figure 5.30 shows a blank form for keeping track of music on compact discs.

Each "field" stores an individual item of data. For example, a database of names and addresses might have fields for first name, last name, address, city, state, and zip code.

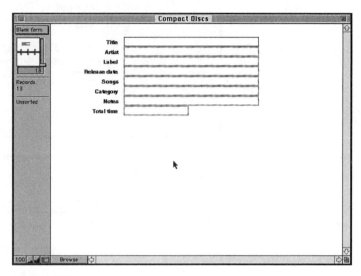

Figure 5.30
Compact disc database form

Entering data is a piece of cake: press the Tab key to move from field to field (or click in the field) and type your data. When you want a new record (a blank form to type in more information), choose **New Record** from the **Edit** menu and off you go.

So far, this isn't all that special. Why not make the list with a word processor or a spreadsheet? Three reasons, which I'll tell you about, and a bunch of others you'll figure out for yourself.

First, FileMaker lets you view your data any way you want. Figures 5.31 and 5.32 show different ways to view the compact disc database: one way for data entry, and another way for viewing artists and titles categories only. You can make as many views (*layouts*) as you want. Figure 5.33 shows FileMaker's layout mode: notice those familiar-looking tools! Yes, you've seen them before, and yes, they work the same way they did before.

The second reason to use FileMaker to keep track of stuff is you can sort things a zillion different ways. Figure 5.34 shows the CD database sorted by category (and displayed in yet a third layout).

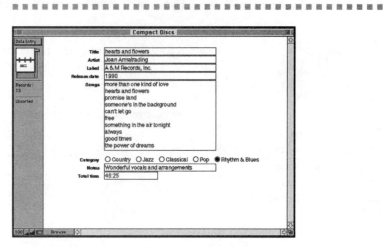

Figure 5.31
Data entry layout

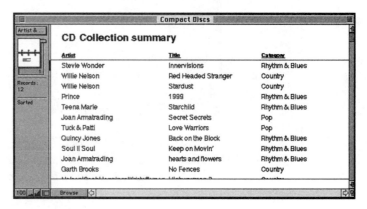

Figure 5.32
Artists, titles, and categories

Tools ——

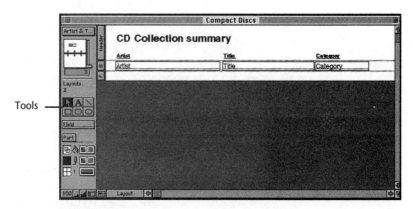

Figure 5.33
FileMaker's Layout mode

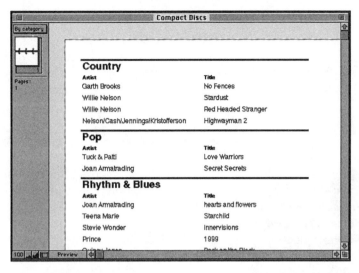

Figure 5.34
CDs sorted by category

n o t E *Using a FileMaker database is easy. Creating one is not so easy. Be sure to read the manuals that come with the program you buy. Or you can always buy a good book, right? Otherwise you'll be stuck with hiring someone (like me) to create the database for you.*

The third reason to use FileMaker to keep track of stuff is it's very easy to find the things you want to find. Suppose you want to make a list of all your Willie Nelson CDs. (A short list? Fine. Suppose *I* want to make a list of all *my* Willie Nelson CDs.) FileMaker's **Find** command lets you do that, winnowing the list down to just what you want. Naturally, you can go back to viewing the entire list in an instant. Figure 5.35 shows FileMaker's Find mode; it really is as easy as it looks.

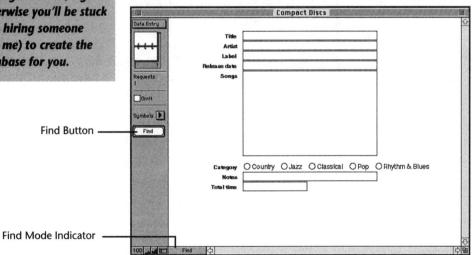

Find Button

Find Mode Indicator

Figure 5.35
Find mode

And now for something completely different.

The programs that appear in the next section are my personal favorites, an elite group that are too useful, elegant, or fun to omit. I strongly urge you to buy everything listed below: these are my all-time Boyce's choices.

All-Time Boyce's Choices

In case you're wondering, I am not paid to write nice things about any program. I wish I were, but I'm not.

Quicken

If you've got a checking account, you've got to have Quicken. It's an electronic checkbook (figure 5.36) and if you can't figure out how to use it on first sight, you are probably having troubles in many other areas of your life as well.

DATE	NUMBER	DESCRIPTION		PAYMENT	✓	DEPOSIT		BALANCE	
		MEMO	CATEGORY						
9/1		Mac book royalties				2,500	00	102,500	00
1993		Yeah, right	Books						
10/1		Mac book royalties				3,500	00	106,000	00
1993		Yeah, right	Books						
11/1		Mac book royalties				6,500	00	112,500	00
1993		Yeah, right	Books						
11/30		Mac book royalties				15,000	00	127,500	00
1993		Yeah, right	Books						
11/30		Mac book royalties				25,000	00	152,500	00
1993		Yeah, right	Books						
12/30		Mac book royalties				10,000	00	162,500	00
1993		Yeah, right	Books						

Swiss Account: Register

Save Restore SPLITS Current Balance: $100,000.00 Ending Balance: $198,500.00

Figure 5.36
Quicken's electronic checkbook

Quicken beats a paper checkbook three ways:

- It never makes mathematical errors.

- It instantly produces reports showing you how much money you spent on office supplies, pizza (same thing), clothes, travel, automobile expenses—you name it.

- It's legible.

The reports alone are worth the price of admission (something like $40), especially at tax time.

Quicken can print checks for you, but you can also use it in conjunction with your paper checks. You'll certainly use Quicken to balance your checkbook—it's a sad commentary on the social life of a struggling author that I *actually look forward* to my monthly reconciliation session. (The fact remains that the system works and I've balanced the books every time.)

I say, get Quicken. It's perfect.

Quicken
Intuit Software
66 Willow Place
Menlo Park, CA 94025
(800) 624-8742

Dynodex

Dynodex is an electronic address book (figure 5.37). It's fast and it prints out about fifty zillion ways. I've used Dynodex for years, and though I keep trying others, I always come back to Dynodex.

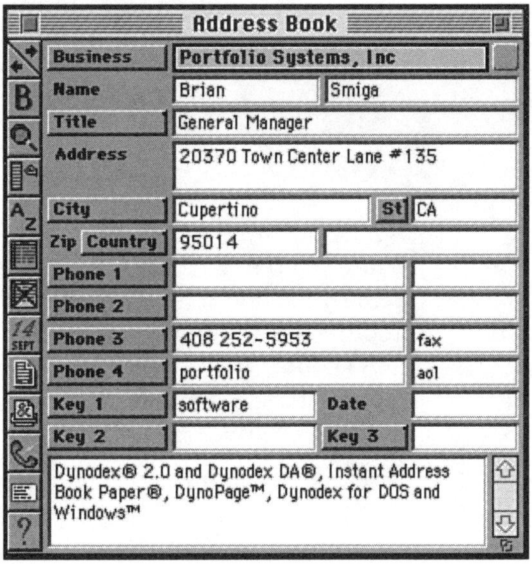

Figure 5.37
Dynodex

For me, an address book can never be fast enough. I want it to open immediately, and I want it to find who I'm looking for immediately. Dynodex comes close.

I realize that you don't need your address book to print fifty zillion ways. You only need it to print *your* way. Well, one of Dynodex's fifty zillion ways probably *is* your way, and if it isn't, you can create your own printing form. Whatever you do, try printing the mini "Dynet" address book: it's as small as a credit card, in teeny-tiny print, on both sides of the paper, and handy as all get-out. I carry mine everywhere.

Naturally Dynodex can do all the things you'd expect it to do, like sorting alphabetically, printing mailing labels, and letting you select everyone who lives in Texas. Dynodex is really a specialized database management system, like something you'd make in FileMaker, only better.

Dynodex hasn't had a major upgrade in a long, long time, but that doesn't indicate neglect. In my view, there's only so much they can do with an address book, and the Dynodex gang's done it. A little cosmetic surgery would be nice, but other than that, Dynodex is just right. Go get it.

Dynodex
Portfolio Systems
20370 Town Center Lane, #135
Cupertino, CA 95014
(800) 729-3966

Now Up-to-Date

Slightly awkward name, but oh, what a calendar. Up-to-Date (figure 5.38) remembers your appointments, reminds you of them by playing sounds and putting up notes (even when the program's not running), and lets you print things out in more than enough ways. Month at a glance, week at a glance, only important appointments, only birthdays, you name it—Now Up-to-Date lets you do it.

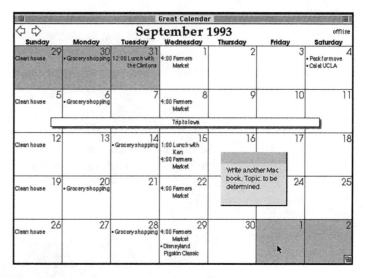

Figure 5.38
Now Up-to-Date

On a network? (If there's more than one of you connected to the printer, you're on a network.) Now Up-to-Date lets you post appointments that everyone can see. Enter "Company Picnic" on *your* calendar and moments later it appears on everyone else's. And no, you don't need a file server or anything else. All you need are the Macs you've already got.

The Now gang realizes that you don't want *all* your appointments posted on everybody's Macs. Thus, they let you categorize your events, and control which categories are public and which are private. You can assign different colors to different categories to make them stand out, and you can choose which categories are visible at any time. None of this is hard to do. You ought to read the manual, but ten minutes with someone who knows the program will teach you the basics.

Now Up-to-Date is the best calendar program there is, by far. Buy it.

▪▪▪▪▪▪▪▪▪▪▪▪▪▪▪▪▪▪▪▪▪▪▪▪▪▪▪▪▪▪▪▪▪▪▪ ▪

Now Software, Inc.
921 SW Washington St., Suite 500
Portland, Oregon 97205-2823
(503) 274-2800

Kid Pix

Kid Pix is a drawing program for kids, or so they say. I think
you'll like it enough that the kids'll be lucky to get anywhere
near it. Figure 5.39 shows the Kid Pix window and a bit of art
by Yours Truly.

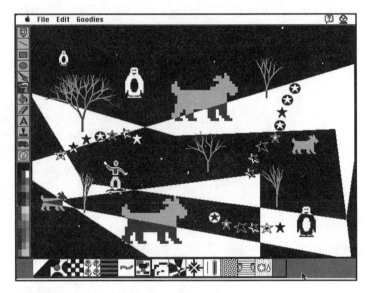

Figure 5.39
Kid Pix

Kid Pix was originally written by a dad for his three-year-old
son. The dad noticed the son's frustration with more complicated programs and decided to make something simple and
fun. He did. There's love and imagination in this program and
it shows.

Using Kid Pix is a gas. Each tool makes a unique noise when
used, and several surprises are there for the finding. My neigh-
bor Miranda likes erasing a picture by dropping a firecracker
on it; figure 5.40 shows what that looks like, but you've got to
hear the Ka-BOOM for yourself.

You can connect your Mac to your stereo using cables from Radio Shack. Properly amplified, Kid Pix can scare the cat. Get a cable with a mini-plug on one end and two male RCAs on the other, and you'll be ready to rock.

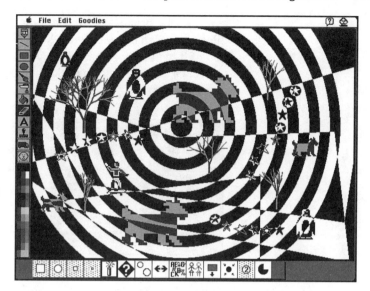

Figure 5.40
Blowing up the picture

I wish Canvas were as much fun. Maybe someone will make "Kid Pix Pro." Meanwhile, get Kid Pix—for your kids, or for yourself.

Kid Pix
Brøderbund Software
17 Paul Drive
San Rafael, CA 94903
(415) 382-4400

Square One

Square One, an application-launching, folder-opening, desktop-neatening file management utility, is elegant, functional, and a doggone pleasure to use. It ought to come with the Mac—it's that good.

Square One lets you create a palette of buttons (figure 5.41) that, when double-clicked, launch programs, open folders, fire up documents, and more. Big deal? You bet. For one thing, it keeps your desktop clean as can be. For another, when you click a Square One button, you're presented with a list of documents you frequently use (figure 5.42); a double-click on a document opens it up, regardless of where the file is actually stored.

Square One acts as a neat and tidy front end to the morass of files squirreled away on your hard disk, and it does such a good job of it, you may forget where you stored your stuff in the first place. Of course, so long as Square One remembers, it really doesn't matter.

Figure 5.41
Square One palette

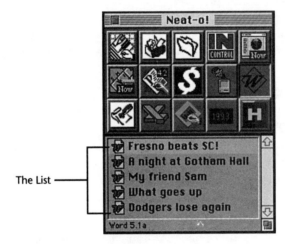

The List

Figure 5.42
List of commonly used files

There are plenty of file-launching utilities, but there's nothing like Square One. Nothing even comes close. When Apple's At Ease program dreams, it dreams that it's Square One.

Square One
Binary Software
2210 Wilshire Boulevard, Suite 900
Santa Monica, CA 90403
(310) 582-8293

Now Utilities

This package of five handy control panels and one nifty application makes using your Mac faster, easier, and basically better. Here's what you get:

WYSIWYG stands for "What you see is what you get." It's pronounced "whizzy-wig." The term came into vogue with the original Macintosh introduction but has faded in popularity. Today's hipper-than-thou Macintosh cognoscenti refer to particularly intuitive and elegant software as "whizzy," but never as "whizzy-wig." Never.

- WYSIWYG Menus, which makes font menus look like figure 5.43 instead of the ordinary figure 5.44.

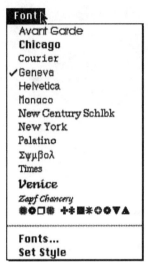

Figure 5.43
With WYSIWYG Menus

Figure 5.44
Without WYSIWYG Menus

- Now Menus, which (among other things) gives your Apple menu little pop-out triangles a la figure 5.45.

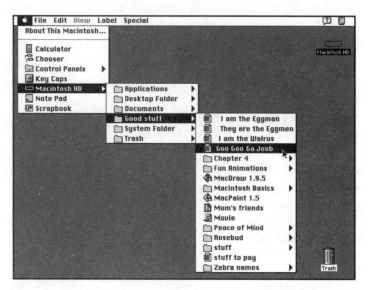

Figure 5.45
With Now Menus

- Now Scrapbook, which beats the tar out of the Mac's standard Scrapbook (figure 5.46) because it lets you see a catalog of your pictures (figure 5.47), then zoom in on the one you want (figure 5.48).

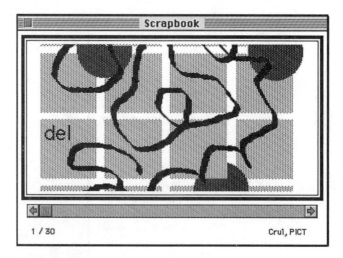

Figure 5.46
The standard Mac Scrapbook

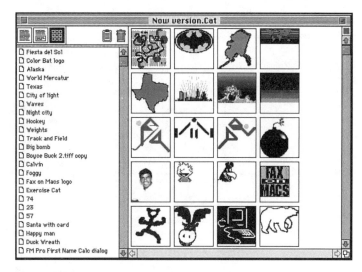

Figure 5.47
The Now Scrapbook catalog view

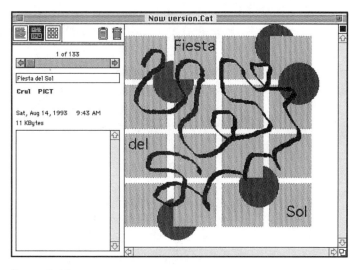

Figure 5.48
The Now Scrapbook actual-size view

- SuperBoomerang, which by some miracle remembers the files and folders you've used most recently and lists them in standard Open… dialog boxes, making it a whole lot easier to find the files again (figure 5.49).

From SuperBoomerang

List of recent files

Figure 5.49
SuperBoomerang

- Startup Manager, which helps you deal with the plethora of extensions and control panels you're sure to acquire.

- Now Save, which automatically saves your work in case you forget to do it yourself.

Now Utilities is a must for the soon-to-be-serious Mac user, and probably useful for the rest of you too. No other collection is anywhere near as good.

Now Software, Inc.
921 SW Washington St., Suite 500
Portland, Oregon 97205-2823
(503) 274-2800

Now Fun

Now Fun is to fun what Now Utilities is to utilities. It gives you options galore for customizing the way your Mac looks and sounds, including:

- FunColors, which enables you to change the color of everything on your Mac—windows, menus, buttons, everything.

- FunPictures, which enables you to use a scanned photo or something you've drawn as a desktop backdrop (figure 5.50).

Figure 5.50
Happenin' backdrop, dude

- FunSounds, which lets you assign sounds such as slamming doors, screaming cats, and howling wolves to events such as starting up, shutting down, ejecting disks, and typing your name.

- FunScreenSavers, which draws pretty pictures on your screen when you're not using it.

- FunCursors, which lets you change the pointer to a flaming torch (figure 5.51) and the watch cursor to a juggler (figure 5.52), among other artistic choices.

Figure 5.51
Flaming Torch pointer cursor

Figure 5.52
Juggler watch cursor

Now Fun thoughtfully provides a way of storing your settings in "sets" so it's easy to switch between a buttoned-down, the-boss-is-watching set and a tie-dyed, nobody-here-but-us-chickens set. Get it, get it, get it.

Now Software, Inc.
921 SW Washington St., Suite 500
Portland, Oregon 97205-2823
(503) 274-2800

Zounds

The obvious question is, if a screen saver starts up in the forest, and there's no one around to hear it, does it make a noise?

Zounds plays sounds in the background, as you work. Unlike screen savers, which are probably playing sounds all night long *while you're not there to listen*, Zounds brightens your day while you're around to appreciate it.

Figure 5.53 shows the Zounds control panel and one of the many possible sound configurations available. Note that these are high-quality, real-life sounds—not synthesized/computerized/homogenized/unrecognized. The crickets sound like crickets, the frogs sound like frogs, and the pond sounds like a pond. You control how frequently the sounds play, and how loudly. This is environmental mood software at its finest. Go now and buy it.

Figure 5.53
Zounds control panel

Zounds
Digital Eclipse Software, Inc.
5515 Doyle Street, Suite 1
Emeryville, CA 94608
(510) 547-6101

Talking Moose

Ah, the Moose. As if I could write a book without mentioning
The King of All Software.

The Talking Moose (figure 5.54) is a control panel that changes
the way people think of their Macs. Put a Moose on a novice's
Mac and watch her face light up. You'll both love it.

Figure 5.54
The Talking Moose

**n
o
t
E** *You can ask the
Moose to proofread
your letters out loud.
It's a riot, and some-
times it actually helps.*

*You can also ask the
Moose to speak the time
every hour; there's
nothing quite like an
animated Moose with a
Canadian accent telling
you, "It's seven o'clock."*

No program does more to give the Mac a personality than the
amazing Mr. Moose. He'll say, "Hello" when you start your Mac
up; he'll say, "Ciao, baby" when you shut your Mac down; he'll
tell you jokes and ask to borrow the car whenever you stop
working long enough. Spend a day watching the Moose and
you'll swear you can read his lips.

Trivial? Maybe. Buy one "for the kids." Or maybe for the
manual, an exercise in clarity and witticism to which your
humble author can only aspire. For my money, anyone who
doesn't like the Moose should have bought an IBM in the first
place.

Absolutely, positively get yourself a Moose. Welcome to the
Club.

Baseline Publishing, Inc.
1770 Moriah Woods Blvd., Suite 14
Memphis, Tennessee 38117-7118
(901) 682-9676

And there you have it: a taste of everything, all in one sitting, and several new ideas on how to spend money. Before moving on, take the mandatory quiz.

1. Do you have an art program?

2. Do you know the difference between paint programs and draw programs?

3. Do you have a page layout program? Do you know what it's for?

4. Do you know what database management programs are for?

5. Do you understand what Square One, Now Utilities, and Now Fun do?

6. Have you already ordered a copy of The Talking Moose? (do not pass "Go" until you've answered this correctly).

Chapter 6
Hardware Buffet

In the last chapter, I told you what software you should buy in order to have "The Complete Mac." Now it's time for the other half of the equation, that being the hardware "goodies" you may want to get. Where possible, I'm naming names: I'll tell you what I like.

(In case you're wondering, the companies mentioned in this book haven't paid for the privilege. Your agent—me—is telling it like it is.)

Cool hardware can make a real difference in your day-to-day work. Here are some of my favorite devices.

Trackballs

A trackball works like a mouse on its back. The ball's on top, and you roll it around with your fingers. Some people hate 'em, some people love 'em; some people say they hate 'em but that's because they haven't tried 'em and they usually end up loving 'em once they finally do.

You can find trackball after trackball advertised in the Mac magazines. Though certainly a personal choice, for my money there's one clear winner, and that's the Kensington Turbo-Mouse. Dumb name, but great product. Here's what I like about it:

- Takes less room on the desk than a mouse

- Large heavy ball rolls extremely smoothly

- Two buttons, easily programmed to do different things (I use the left one like a mouse's button and the right one to lock down, for dragging things)

- Same color and style as the Mac keyboard

The word "hardware" was around long before computers. "Software" was coined to denote the nebulous idea of computer programs in general. "Firmware", a term you hardly hear, describes software that's permanently written onto a piece of hardware. Instructions on a chip are firmware. Another firmware example: the "Welcome to Macintosh" message that appears every time you start your Mac. Yet another word to throw around at the office party.

nOtE *If you've got a PowerBook, you've got one of the most awkward trackballs ever pushed upon a defenseless public. I can't say enough rotten things about the PowerBook's trackball. What a dog.*

You can connect a TurboMouse (or any other trackball, or a mouse for that matter) to a PowerBook if the built-in trackball drives you nuts. I'd park a TurboMouse on my desk and plug my PowerBook into it, if in fact I had a PowerBook. Nice to know that I'll know what to do in case I ever get one!

n
o *Most inkjet printers,*
t *the Hewlett-Packards*
E *included, aren't PostScript printers. For printing graphics, this is an important difference, but for printing text, it's not. You'll have to decide for yourself how important PostScript capabilities are. If money is an object, and if you print mostly letters and memos and such, an inkjet printer is an excellent choice.*

- Extra connector lets you attach your mouse to the trackball in case you still want to use it

- Quality construction

The Kensington does everything right. I didn't think I'd ever use a trackball, but a couple of days with the TurboMouse changed my mind. Get one.

Printers

Everybody either wants or needs a printer. Sure, you can save some money by poor-boying your work to someone else's printer, but it's nicer to have your own.

Apple makes many printers. So does Hewlett-Packard and so do many other manufacturers. The bad news is all these choices make it hard to decide. The good news is there are good choices no matter how much money you decide to spend.

Printers can be separated into two categories: PostScript printers, which generally cost a lot but print fabulously, and QuickDraw printers, which generally cost less and print pretty darned well to boot. Within these categories you'll find printers classified according to the technology they use to print the page; the most common printer technologies are dot matrix, inkjet, and laser.

Dot matrix printers aren't very cool. They're noisy and their output is coarse compared to everything else. Inkjet printers, on the other hand, are quiet, make terrific output, and start at something like $300 (which is roughly what dot matrix printers cost). The best inkjet printers are from Hewlett-Packard (though there's one from Apple—the black-and-white StyleWriter II— that's close). I'd rate them this way: the Hewlett-Packard DeskWriter 550C (*color* inkjet); the regular Hewlett-Packard DeskWriter (black and white inkjet); and the Apple StyleWriter II (black and white inkjet). All are terrific printers and terrific values. I'd get the 550C if I had the money. Please, do not send cash through the mail.

Laser printers, once the ultimate Macintosh status symbols, are now affordable for everyone (save the occasional Mac author who writes out of the goodness of his heart, a deep sense of moral obligation, and a spirit of charity and benevolence toward his brother and sister Mac users).

Cheap laser printers come without PostScript, meaning they're great for text, but not quite as great for graphics. These printers are typically less than $1,000. Better laser printers include PostScript, which helps the graphics and adds to the price. These printers are typically between $1,000 and $1,500.

Generally speaking, spending more money on a laser printer gets you a faster printer with better output (though even the cheapos print a pretty fine page). In my book (and this *is* my book), your printer can never be fast enough.

You probably already knew this, but the word "modem" is actually a contraction of "Modulator-Demodulator." The modulation they're talking about is the process of changing computer information into sound (which is the only thing phone lines can carry).

Of course, there's always the chance that "modem" showed up in the modem inventor's alphabet soup one day, and with the good names already taken, he went with it. Either story is so far-fetched that you will probably get away with using one during your favorite know-it-all-show-off session.

Modems

Modems are the least-understood computer accessory ever made. Few people know what they're for. Which is too bad, because modems let you do cool things.

Modems, to computers, are like telephones to people (and they're roughly the same size, as well). They let computers communicate (figure 6.1) over great distances, over phone lines, just as you'd chat with your friend in Puerto Rico from your own place in Beverly Hills.

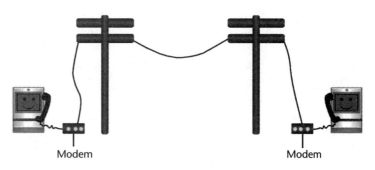

Modem   Modem

Figure 6.1
Macs using a modem to communicate

You can use a modem to send a file across town or across the country in minutes, but with Federal Express so easy and quick, and with fax machines all over the place, I don't think it's worth the trouble. You probably won't either.

Where modems shine is in letting you connect to great big computers, called *online services* and *bulletin boards*, such as America Online and CompuServe. These services (for a fee) enable you to send electronic mail to anyone else with a

**n
O
t
E** *You can reach me on
America Online by
sending mail to
"christianb."*

*"Freeware" is software that
you can use for free. This
doesn't mean that its
worthless however; you'd
be surprised how much
good freeware is out there.
"Shareware" is software
that you can try before you
buy; this means you can get
it and use it before you pay
for it. The programmer sets
a shareware fee that he
requests you send in if you
like and will continue to
use the software.
"Updates" are supposedly-
minor revisions that
enhance or improve
programs that already
work. "Bug fixes" are
supposedly-minor revisions
that fix programs that
didn't work. Sometimes it's
hard to tell these two
apart.*

modem and a computer—the computer doesn't even have to be
a Mac, and it doesn't even have to be on when you send the
mail. Many computer luminaries respond more quickly to
electronic mail than to regular in-an-envelope-and-don't-
forget-the-stamp *snail mail*. Additionally, since you can make
general pleas for help (rather than address your plea to a single
person), literally zillions of people will see your message and it's
likely that several will answer.

Most bulletin boards and online services also include large
collections of software. You'll find freeware, shareware, updates,
bug fixes, and demonstration versions of many programs.

All you do is ask for the software—the computer on the other
end squirts it through its modem, onto the phone line, into your
modem, then into your Mac. Without the modem, the transfer
wouldn't work, and THAT's why we have to have modems.

Hopefully I've convinced you that modems are cool. Now you
need to figure out which one to buy. My favorite modems are
the ones from Global Village, a company that makes nothing
but modems and does a darned good job of it. All of their
modems come with nifty software that lets you fax (yes, I said
FAX) to *any* fax machine or computer (also equipped with a fax
modem) directly from any Macintosh program, directly from
your Macintosh. You don't have to print, or watch your fax
machine jam, or anything. Just press a button and the document faxes away.

Personally, I use the modem more to send faxes than I do to
transfer data, mostly because sending faxes is easier. Which-
ever modem you end up getting, be sure it can handle faxing.
It's cool. Figure on spending between $200 and $400, depending on the speed of the modem (faster is better, but remember:
"even a slow modem's better than no modems").

The Buffet is Now Closed

With all these hot hardware choices, you're probably getting
full. That's all right, because with these selections from the
buffet, you'll have about all you could ever need (well, at least
all we've got time to cover here). With all this hardware, and
the software from chapter 5, you're all set to do lots of good
work and have fun at the same time. What a deal! Next, we'll

note

In many cases, it's easier—not to mention faster—to get your updates and bug fixes via modem than by calling the company on the phone. Nearly everyone in the Mac business participates in this sort of software distribution.

tackle all the stuff you need to know about the mysterious System Folder. But first, here's your quiz:

1. Do you know the difference between hardware, software, and firmware?

2. Are you going to try a trackball? Do you know which one I prefer?

3. Do you know your basic printer options? Which type is the best? Which one has low cost, but still does a good job? Which type should you avoid like the plague?

4. Can you baffle people with stories of the origin of the word "modem?"

5. Are we having fun yet?

Chapter 7
The System Folder

Every Mac has a System Folder (figure 7.1), but no one seems to know why. That's OK, because the System Folder does its work behind the scenes and you can get by without knowing more than that. However, if you want to control your Mac, to make it act the way you want it to, you need to know this stuff. This chapter introduces you to the System Folder and what you find inside it. First, a brief discussion of the nature of the System Folder: what it does, and how.

Figure 7.1
The System Folder

> **note**
>
> *That little Mac symbol on the System Folder is sort of like the "S" on Superman's chest. It tells you that this is something special. As with Superman, there's only one System Folder, or should be.*

The Nature of the System Folder

There's a lot more to your Macintosh than meets the eye. You probably think that you communicate directly with the Mac, that when you say "Save this file" or "Make this bold," your Macintosh says, "Okay." That's not really how it works.

Everything you do with a Macintosh involves you and an application. You already know that applications are computer programs such as Word, Excel, ClarisWorks, and FileMaker, but you probably don't already know that applications are doing a lot of work behind the scenes. In fact, when you tell your application to do something, the application doesn't do it. Instead, the application translates your request into something the Macintosh's operating system can understand, completely

note *Software companies upgrade their products all the time for other reasons, too—the most common being to give them a chance to ask you to pony up some more bucks. Be aware that there are no laws against using non-current versions of software. Don't automatically upgrade if the old stuff's working for you.*

Most people refer to Systems 7.0, 7.0.1, and 7.1 as System 7, and it's fine with me if they do. These Systems are very similar (all System 6 versions were more or less alike, too). The big differences are between System 6 in general and System 7 in general. Someday there will be a System 8, with variations such as System 8.0.1, etc., and you can be sure that it will be quite different from today's System 7.

passing the buck. The operating system then translates the application's request into something the Macintosh's hardware can understand. The hardware does the work, and when it's done, sends a message back up the line to the operating system. The operating system tells the application, and the application tells you.

Thus, there are a couple of translations going on every time you want to do something. The better the translations, the easier it is for you. That's why applications are upgraded all the time—the newer versions are better at translating your wishes into commands the operating system can handle.

It makes some sense to think that a better operating system would make things better too. Since everything that happens on your Mac has to pass through the operating system, an operating system with more capabilities would allow applications to deliver more complicated commands (and consequently would allow you to tell your applications to do more complicated things). In fact, the operating system is frequently updated, just as an application is. The current version is called "System 7.1."

So where's the operating system live?

Good question. The operating system lives in the System Folder (Aha!), but not entirely. Part of the operating system is stored on computer chips inside your Mac. It's the combination of the stuff in the System Folder and the stuff on the chips that make up the operating system. We can't do much to the stuff on the chips (it's firmware remember?), but we can do *a lot* to the stuff in the System Folder. And why would you want to do something to the stuff in the System Folder? To make your Mac behave the way you want it to. That, my friend, is what this chapter's about. Knowledge is power, and all that.

You've seen one part of the System Folder already, and it happened without your doing anything. That part is the Finder, and we'll look at it again right now.

The Finder

The Finder (figure 7.2) is the most under-appreciated piece of software ever to grace a Mac. Not the most *un*appreciated (there's a lot of doggy software that shouldn't be appreciated at all); *under*-appreciated.

Finder

Figure 7.2
The Finder

The chips we mentioned earlier are called "Read-Only Memory," or "ROM," chips. Newer Macs have more of the operating system stored permanently on ROM chips than older ones do. Remember though, that it's the combination of the stuff on the chips and the stuff in the System Folder that makes up an operating system. Thus, older Macs store a larger percentage of the operating system in their System Folders than newer Macs do. This isn't all that important, but it's good to know the truth.

So what does the Finder do? The obvious answer ("it finds things") is only partly true. The Finder's real job is *file management*, a high-falutin' way of saying it keeps track of stuff on your hard disk and makes it easy for you to retrieve it. When you double-click on a folder icon, it's the Finder that makes the icon fly open into a window, and it's the Finder that puts the right stuff into the window. When you throw something into the Trash, remember that it's the Finder that put the Trash there. When you drag a document from one folder to another, it's the Finder that handles the actual moving of the file. Basically, if it has to do with moving files around, or renaming them, or folders, or the Trash, the Finder's responsible.

Clearly you've been using the Finder all along (the Mac turns the Finder on as soon as you start up your Mac). Knowing that the Mac has the Finder isn't going to change anything. But knowing that the Finder has some powerful capabilities might. Here are some of them.

Pop-Out Folders

One of the Mac's best features is that you can open as many windows as you wish. One of the Mac's *worst* features is that you can open as many windows as you wish. When you start hunting around for something, opening folder after folder, it's easy to make a pretty big mess (figure 7.3). It doesn't take long before things get out of hand.

Fortunately, someone has thought this out and given us another way to handle things. That way is via *pop-out folders*.

Pop-out folders provide a kind of outlining feature, letting you see inside folders without opening them into windows. Figure 7.4 shows a folder popped out.

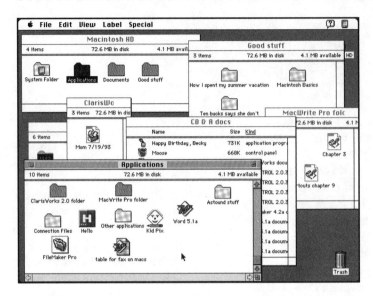

Figure 7.3
What a mess!

Figure 7.4
A popped out folder

See that little triangle next to the folder called "More stuff?" If I click on it once, it pops out to a third level (figure 7.5). Click on a downward-pointing triangle and the folder "unpops," collapsing back to normal.

It doesn't take long to get more stuff popped open than you'd ever want to close. Try this all-time cool tip for collapsing every folder within a single window:

1. *Be sure the window is active (has stripes across the top). If it doesn't, click on it.*

2. *Press Command-A (for Select All). (Look in the Edit menu if you don't believe me.)*

3. *Press Command-left arrow (the cursor key). Everything collapses. Very, very cool. I do this all the time.*

Figure 7.5
Popped out to a third level

Here's some stuff to know. First, you can't pop out anything if you're viewing your files by icon or by small icon. You need to be viewing things by name, date, size, label, or kind. Take a trip to the **View** menu and choose one of those now.

Second, you can't pop out anything that isn't a folder. This might not be a big surprise to you but it might be to someone else.

Third, too much of a good thing is a bad thing. It's easy to pop open so many folders that your Mac gets totally bogged down displaying that single jumbo window. Remember, the more stuff the Mac has to display, the longer it's going to take. Don't pop open everything under the sun.

Aliases

Aliases are tres cool. They'll change your life. They'll make you richer, thinner, and a better dancer.

Actually, they probably won't do those things. But they will make your Mac life nicer.

I guess telling you what an alias is would help. Apple calls them "pointers" which does nothing for me. I call them "remote controls." See if you don't agree.

Consider the lowly TV remote control. What do we know about it?

- The remote control enables you to start the TV without actually touching the TV.

- The remote control is not the TV. It only controls the TV.

- Losing the remote control isn't as bad as losing the TV.

- The remote control doesn't take up as much space as the TV does.

- Throwing away the remote control doesn't throw away the TV, and vice versa.

- It's possible to have several remote controls for a single TV, conveniently scattered about so you've always got one handy.

Believe it or not, you can substitute "alias" for "remote control" and "document/application/folder" for "TV" and the statements will still be true.

So where do you get these aliases? From the Finder, that's where. Take a look at the **File** menu (figure 7.6). See that **Make Alias** command? That's the one for us. Let's try it out.

```
File
New Folder     ⌘N
Open           ⌘O
Print          ⌘P
Close Window   ⌘W

Get Info       ⌘I
Sharing...
Duplicate      ⌘D
Make Alias
Put Away       ⌘Y

Find...        ⌘F
Find Again     ⌘G

Page Setup...
Print Desktop...
```

Figure 7.6
Make Alias command in the **File** menu

Suppose you want a remote control (an alias) for your word processor. You could stash the remote somewhere convenient, making it easier to get to than the real thing is. When you double-click on the alias, the alias will send the signal to your word processor, and the word processor will start itself up.

1. Find your word processor. That is, dig around in your folders until the word processor is showing (figure 7.7).

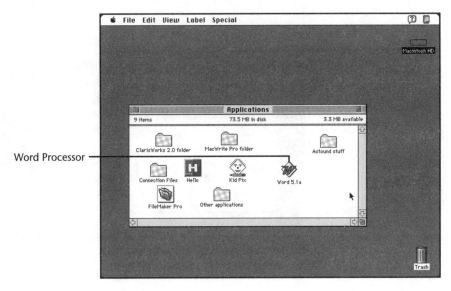

Word Processor

Figure 7.7
Word processor showing

2. Click once on the word processor's icon. *Don't click twice!* If
    you do, you'll launch the word processor and you'll have
    to quit and start over.

3. Choose **Make Alias** from the **File** menu.

    You'll see a new icon called "*Word alias*" or something
    similar (figure 7.8). Notice that the name is italicized—
    your clue that this is an alias and not a "real" word
    processor. The word "alias" at the end of the name should
    tip you off, too.

That's all there is to it. A double-click on the alias yields the
same result as a double-click on the real word processor. Move
the alias to the Desktop (just drag it there), as I've done in
figure 7.9. Close up all your windows and try the alias. Believe
me, it'll work.

Those of you too smart for your own good are probably thinking, "Why not just move the real word processor's icon to the
Desktop? Why deal with the alias at all?" Because, my nearly-
but-not-quite-correct student, the word processor needs to be
stored with its dictionaries and other supplemental files. Moving the real word processor would make it stop working, or at
least lead to a host of other problems. The alias technique lets
you arrange things the way the Mac likes them while simultaneously arranging the same things (through aliases) the way
you like them. It's very cool.

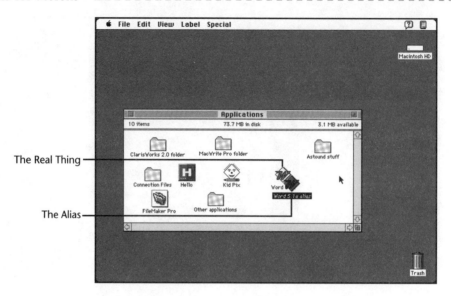

The Real Thing ———

The Alias ———

Figure 7.8
Word and *Word alias*

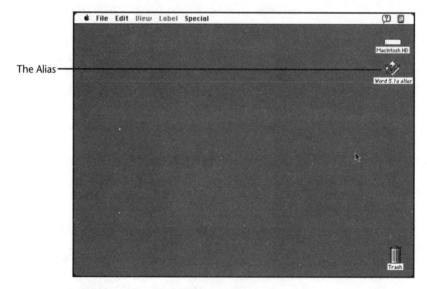

The Alias ———

Figure 7.9
Alias on the Desktop

Not convinced? Try this:

1. Click on the real word processor icon.

2. Choose **Get Info** from the **File** menu.

Notice how much space the real word processor takes on the disk. Figure 7.10 shows what you get when you get info for Microsoft Word version 5.1.

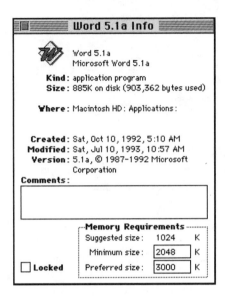

Figure 7.10
Info for the real word processor

Now **Get Info** for the alias. Same drill as before: Click on the icon and choose **Get Info** from the **File** menu. Figure 7.11 shows what I got.

Compare figures 7.10 and 7.11. Notice that the alias takes up almost no space at all, especially compared to the real word processor. Notice also that the alias's Kind is "alias" and the real word processor's Kind is "application." Finally, notice that the bottoms of the Get Info boxes are different.

I hope I've nipped in the bud any thoughts of simply duplicating the real word processor and scattering them about the desktop. That method will work, but it takes a lot of disk space to accomplish. Don't do it.

n
o *In case you don't see*
t *why, here's why.*
E *Duplicate files are*
great, but they're not
duplicates as soon as
you change one. There's
absolutely no way to
reconcile two formerly-
identical files that have
been modified sepa-
rately. What you have
then are two slightly
different files, neither
of which is completely
correct. It's a major
drag.

Naturally the extra disk
space needed to store
duplicate files is
another disadvantage,
but I think the "not
duplicates for long"
disadvantage should be
enough to convince
you. Hope so.

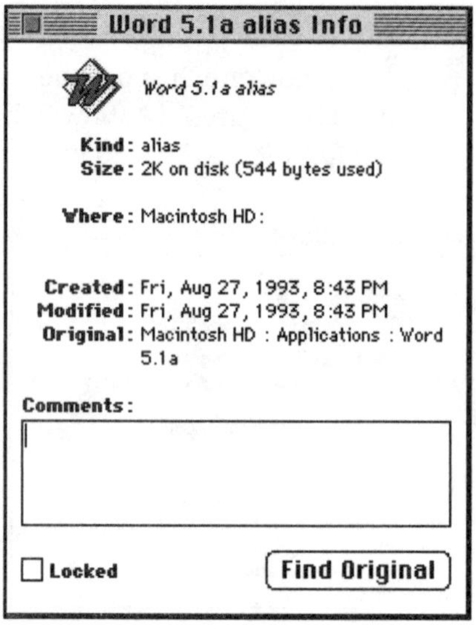

Figure 7.11
Info for the alias

You can make aliases for files, too. Suppose you write letters to some friends. Do you store the letters in the same folder as the word processor you used, or do you store them somewhere else? It might make sense to make a "Correspondence" folder, but then again, it might make sense to store the letters in folders customized for each friend. You can't save the real thing in all three places, and duplicating the real thing leads to major trouble (you'd have three different versions as soon as you started editing). What you need are *aliases*: Put the real file somewhere (anywhere!), and then put aliases to it in every folder you think you'd ever want them in. Now, no matter where you look, you'll find either the original file, or an *alias* to the original file. Double-clicking on the original opens the original—and so does double-clicking on an alias. This beats the tar out of putting duplicates of files all over the place. I hope you see why.

Here are a couple of rules about aliases. Be sure you understand them.

- Alias names are always italicized.

- Renaming an alias does not hurt anything.

- Renaming the original document/folder/application doesn't hurt anything, either.

- Moving the alias doesn't hurt anything.

- Moving the original doesn't hurt anything, either.

- Trashing an alias does not trash the original.

- Trashing the original does not trash the alias. (However, an alias without an original is worthless.)

Finding Things

Note the command-key shortcut, Command-F. This is one that makes sense.

It's more than frustrating to lose a document somewhere on the hard disk. Yet it happens to nice people all the time. Apple knows this, which is why they built a "find" capability into the System 7 Finder. Figure 7.12 shows the **Find...** command in the Finder's **File** menu.

File	
New Folder	⌘N
Open	⌘O
Print	⌘P
Close Window	⌘W
Get Info	⌘I
Sharing...	
Duplicate	⌘D
Make Alias	
Put Away	⌘Y
Find...	⌘F
Find Again	⌘G
Page Setup...	
Print Desktop...	

Figure 7.12
Choosing **Find...** from the **File** menu

When you choose **Find...** or hit Command-F, you get a dialog box like the one shown in figure 7.13. If you're looking for a document called "Letter to Larry," you type that in (figure 7.14) and press the Find button. Your Mac will chug along and eventually, if it finds what you're looking for, it will display the icon (highlighted). Note that the Mac will open the appropriate folder as necessary to display the file's icon (figure 7.15).

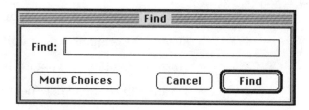

Figure 7.13
Find... dialog box

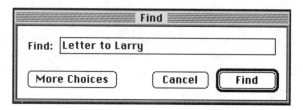

Figure 7.14
Where's Larry?

*If the file you want is
called "Memo to Larry" or
"Larry Letter" or "Larry
9/15," you aren't going to
find it by asking for "Letter
to Larry." The smart thing
to do is search for only the
stuff you're absolutely sure
of. In this case, searching
for "Larry" would be the
best idea.*

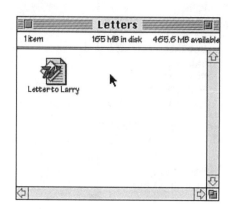

Figure 7.15
Larry found

If you find the wrong file, you've got a couple of choices.
One choice is to choose **Find Again** from the **File** menu
(fig-ure 7.16).

The Command-key shortcut for Find Again is Command-G. Think of it as Guess Again and maybe it'll be easier to remember.

File	
New Folder	⌘N
Open	⌘O
Print	⌘P
Close Window	⌘W
Get Info	⌘I
Sharing...	
Duplicate	⌘D
Make Alias	
Put Away	⌘Y
Find...	⌘F
Find Again	⌘G
Page Setup...	
Print Desktop...	

Figure 7.16
Choosing **Find Again** from the **File** menu

You can use **Find Again** over and over (and it's a lot nicer to do it if you're using Command-G instead of the mouse). Keep pressing Command-G until the right file appears. Notice that the Mac will open *and close* windows as necessary. This is a Very Nice Feature.

If Command-G (**Find Again**) doesn't do it for you, try pressing the More Choices button in the **Find...** dialog box (figure 7.17). Doing so leads to an expanded **Find...** dialog box (figure 7.18).

More Choices button ——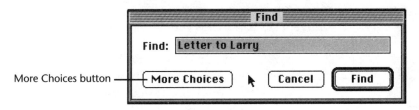

Figure 7.17
The More Choices button

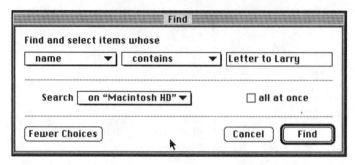

Figure 7.18
After clicking on the More Choices button

Ask and ye shall receive! Dig these crazy choices: You can search for items by name, of course, but also by creation date, modification date, kind, and more. Figure 7.19 shows the list of options when searching by file name.

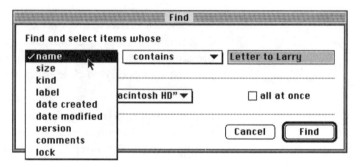

Figure 7.19
Different kinds of things you can search for.

The pop-up menu next to the "all at once" checkbox has an option to search only the currently selected items, which leads to some

In figure 7.19, notice the innocuous little checkbox, "all at once." Check this and your Mac finds everything that matches your request, then (making effective use of pop-out folders) highlights them all at once. This makes it easy to find that letter to Larry, even if all you remember about it is that you created it last Thursday. Just set up the search to find documents created on the desired date, check "all at once," and then click on the Find button. Sure, you'll probably find more than one item, but scanning through the highlighted ones is a lot easier and faster than scanning through everything. The found set of items (folders, documents, applications, whatever) will remain highlighted as long as you don't click on something that's not highlighted.

interesting possibilities. For example, you could search for all documents with the word "Larry" in their titles and have the Mac display them "all at once." They'll be selected, and stay that way until you select something else; thus, if you then tell your Mac to search "the selected items" for documents created on a certain date, you'll end up with exactly the thing you're looking for. Get good at this now, before you're desperate to find something. That's not the time to learn.

The Finder's got some other tricks up its sleeve, but they're perfectly explained already. Choose **Finder Shortcuts** from the **Balloon Help** menu (figure 7.20) and you'll see what I mean.

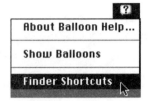

Figure 7.20
Finder Shortcuts

The Apple Menu Items Folder

The **Apple** menu (figure 7.21) is always the first menu on the left, regardless of what you're doing. You'll see the **Apple** menu whether you're using Microsoft Word, ClarisWorks, Aldus PageMaker, or whatever, and (until you make changes) you'll always see the same items in it.

note *The first item in the Apple menu has something to do with the program you're currently using. Thus, you'll see "About Microsoft Word" at the top when using Word, "About ClarisWorks" when you're using ClarisWorks, and so on. Sometimes you'll find some program-specific help or other program-specific items near the top as well.*

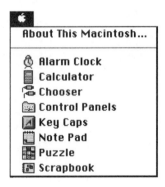

Figure 7.21
Standard **Apple** menu

GENIUS TIP

Not sure which program you're currently using? Use the Application menu (Chapter 2, remember?).

Apple puts some interesting and useful items into the **Apple** menu for you (we'll play with some soon). Since the **Apple** menu is always visible, you can always get to the items in the menu. (This is quite different from most menus, which are totally program-specific.)

Three of my favorite **Apple** menu items are the Calculator, Key Caps, and the Scrapbook. Let's take a look.

The Calculator

The Calculator (figure 7.22) isn't very fancy but it does the job. Try it yourself: Just select **Calculator** from the **Apple** menu and there it is. You can click on the Calculator's buttons with the mouse, or (better yet) use your keyboard's numeric keypad. Would you believe that the Calculator and the numeric keypad are laid out in the same arrangement? What a coincidence!

Figure 7.22
The Calculator

This is great, of course, so long as you know how to use it. Naturally you won't have a chance unless you're a computer programmer (and the odds of that aren't good). The tricky parts are the asterisk, which (to a programmer) means "multiply" and the slash, which (also to a programmer) means "divide." Why we can't have the traditional "x" and "÷" instead of dorky computer programmer symbols is a mystery for the ages, especially considering they call the Mac "the computer for the rest of us." (One other tricky part involves the keypad's Enter key. Think of it as another equals sign and you'll have it made.)

Key Caps

How many fonts does your Mac have? How can you type an apple (), or an upside-down question mark (¿), or a copyright symbol (©)? How do you know what each font looks like? The answer to all three questions involves the very handy Key Caps (figure 7.23).

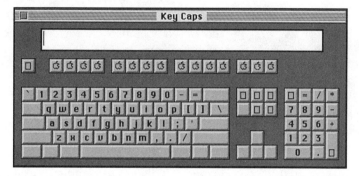

Figure 7.23
Key Caps

Choose **Key Caps** from the **Apple** menu. Notice that a new menu, called **Key Caps**, appears to the right in the menu bar. The **Key Caps** menu contains every font installed on your Macintosh (you'll learn to install fonts later in this chapter). Choose a font and watch what happens to the Key Caps window. Figure 7.24 shows the Key Caps window after choosing **Helvetica**. As you can see, the Key Caps window is displayed in Helvetica as soon as you choose that font.

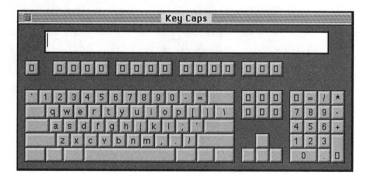

Figure 7.24
After choosing Helvetica

Now hold a Shift key down. Notice anything? The Key Caps display changes to upper case! This may be the clue you need to discover that the Key Caps display is exactly the same as your keyboard. When you hold the Shift key down, you see (on the screen) what each key does when you press it in conjunction with the Shift key.

Better yet: Hold an Option key down. Wow... funky symbols. Now you know how to type those copyright symbols (hold Option and press "g"). Lastly, hold the Option and the Shift down. You get *more* characters! In fact, every font has four sets of characters:

- The regular set
- The Shift set
- The Option set
- The Shift-Option set

You don't always get four characters out of every key. Some keys don't do anything when you press the Option or the Option-Shift combination. Hollow rectangles in the Key Caps display indicate missing or undefined characters.

On the brighter side, Key Caps gives you a facility for determining how to type the proper pictures in fonts such as Cairo and Mobile (figure 7.25).

note

Some fonts have additional key sets hidden away. Try holding the Control key with the Key Caps window open. See anything? Depending on the font you've chosen, you might.

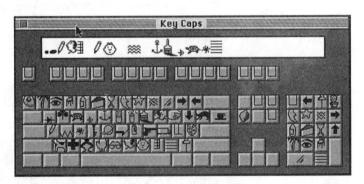

Figure 7.25
Cairo, revealed

Remember, Key Caps (like everything in the **Apple** menu) is available all the time. So, when you're writing with ClarisWorks (or anything else) and you're wondering how to type a cent sign (¢), get to Key Caps and look it up. You don't have to quit the writing program to get to Key Caps—it's always there.

The Scrapbook

Way back when (actually, in Chapter 3) we learned to cut, copy, and paste, and that was pretty powerful. The Scrapbook adds to that by providing a permanent place to store pictures, text, and sounds. The idea is you'll build a library (a scrapbook) of frequently-needed items and have them handy for subsequent pasting. Here's how it works.

1. Launch your word processor.

2. Choose **Scrapbook** from the **Apple** menu.

   Your screen should look something like figure 7.26.

3. Scroll through the Scrapbook's pages using the arrows at the bottom of the Scrapbook's window. When you find something you like, stop.

4. Choose **Copy** from the **Edit** menu, or press Command-C.

5. Close the Scrapbook by clicking on its Close box.

6. Click in your word processing document and choose **Paste** from the **Edit** menu (Command-V works, too).

How about that! The stuff you copied from the Scrapbook really did get pasted into your document.

Putting things into your Scrapbook is just as easy. Suppose you've created a spiffy picture and you want to be able to copy and paste it into various letters to friends. The idea is simple:

1. Select the picture by clicking on it or dragging through it. Which method you use depends on the program you're using.

2. **Copy** it.

3. Choose **Scrapbook** from the **Apple** menu.

4. Paste.

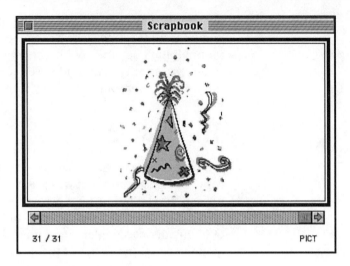

Figure 7.26
The Scrapbook

That's it. Notice that the bottom of the Scrapbook window indicates how many items are in the Scrapbook and how far along you are. Also notice that your new Scrapbook item (your picture) is on its own page, a new page automatically added by the Scrapbook when you said **Paste**.

This is a good time to list some Scrapbook Rules:

- The Scrapbook is permanent. It survives restarting and shutting down the Mac.

- The Scrapbook always adds a new page when you paste something into it.

- The Scrapbook has unlimited capacity, page-wise. One hundred pages is nothing remarkable.

- Copying a Scrapbook item leaves the original untouched. Cutting removes it (so does clearing, but you can't paste if you clear).

- Sometimes the Scrapbook doesn't display the whole item you pasted into it. Don't sweat it—things will probably work out fine anyhow. The hard part, of course, is figuring out what something is when you can't see it.

GENIUS TIP

What happens when you copy or cut, but don't use the scrapbook? I'm glad you asked. Whatever you copy or cut is stored on the clipboard that is the part of the Mac's operating system and stores whatever you cut or copy.

There are two major limitations to the clipboard. First, it only holds one item at a time. So if you cut once and then cut again without a paste between them, you can say, "Hasta la Vista, Baby" to the first item. It's gone. Second, the clipboard is cleared whenever you shut down or restart the Mac.

Use the clipboard for temporary items (moving around, repeating text, and so on). Use the scrapbook for things you want to keep.

Well, so. You know that the **Apple** menu, straight from the factory, comes loaded with nifty stuff. But that's not the half of it. The really great thing about the **Apple** menu is you can add things to it yourself. What kinds of things? Oh, how about your favorite applications? How about the address book you're always using? How about that folder of correspondence that you hate to go digging for? All these things, and more, are easily inserted into the **Apple** menu.

Adding items to the **Apple** menu is a snap once you know how. The key is the Apple Menu Items folder (figure 7.27), located in the System Folder.

Apple Menu Items

Figure 7.27
Apple Menu Items folder

Open up your Apple Menu Items folder. View the contents by Name (use the **Views** menu). Now look at the **Apple** menu. Notice the similarity? Figure 7.28 shows how it looks over here.

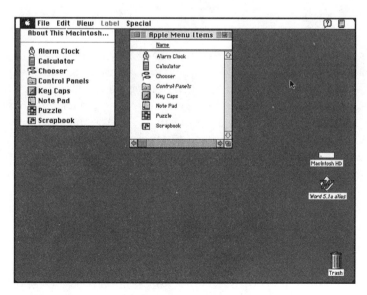

Figure 7.28
Apple menu and Apple Menu Items folder

GENIUS TIP

Don't put "real" things into the Apple Menu Items folder. Use aliases instead. That way, you can leave your hard disk arranged the way it currently is and also provide easy access through the Apple Menu. Make aliases of the things you use the most, and toss the aliases into the Apple Menu Items folder. They'll instantly appear in the Apple Menu (no restarting required).

note *Funny thing about aliases. They're italicized, except when they're in the Apple menu. They look normal in there. No matter, just one for you to chew on.*

Basically, anything in the Apple Menu Items folder appears in the **Apple** menu. As an experiment, drag the Calculator out of the Apple Menu Items folder and put it on the Desktop. Now look at the **Apple** menu. The Calculator isn't in the menu anymore, is it? Now drag the Calculator back to the Apple Menu Items folder. Check the **Apple** menu. The Calculator is back where it belongs.

It turns out that there's nothing all that special about the items Apple put into the **Apple** menu. You can put anything you want into it.

One last thing about the **Apple** menu. It's sorted alphabetically, so if you want an item to appear at the top you'll have to rename the item. Just go to the Apple Menu Items folder, find the right icon, and do it. The easiest way to pull this off is to add a space before an alias's name (in the **Apple** menu alphabet, spaces come before letters and numbers, so items with leading spaces are at or near the top of the list when sorted by name). Don't worry about running out of room in the **Apple** menu, either; you get 52 items, which should be enough. That many makes for a pretty long menu.

The Control Panels Folder

You've learned how to customize the **Apple** menu. Now you'll learn how to customize your entire Mac. It's easy and fun. I mean it. Here you'll learn to change the beep sound, change the way icons look in Finder windows, change the way your screen displays, and change the pattern on your desktop. All of these (and more) are controlled by little panels called—dig this—*control panels*. It turns out that control panels are stored in—double-dig *this*—the Control Panels folder. It's enough to restore your faith after that Calculator multiplication and division fiasco.

Sound

You probably noticed that your Mac beeps at you when you make mistakes. This beeping is controlled by the Sound control panel. Naturally the Sound control panel resides in the Control

Panels folder; let's open the folder, then we'll play with the sound. (Apple made it easy for you to get to the Control Panels folder—they put an alias to the real folder into the **Apple** menu.)

1. Choose **Control Panels** from the **Apple** menu (figure 7.29).

   The Control Panels folder opens into a window.

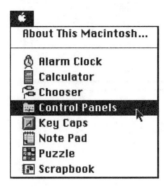

Figure 7.29
Choosing **Control Panels** from the **Apple** menu

2. Find the Sound control panel icon (figure 7.30).

Figure 7.30
Sound control panel icon

3. Double-click on the Sound control panel.

   You get a window like figure 7.31.

4. Adjust the volume by dragging the slider up or down.

   (Setting the volume to zero turns the sound completely off. Instead, the menu bar will flash every time the Mac wants to beep.)

5. Choose a sound by clicking on one in the list. When you're happy, close the Sound control panel and get back to work.

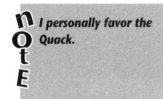
I personally favor the Quack.

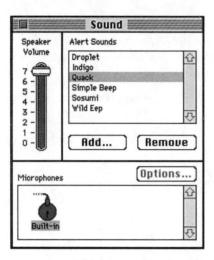

Figure 7.31
The Sound control panel

Views

(I never tire of showing this one. For some reason, no one figures it out on their own, so it's always impressive when I demo it.)

The Views control panel (figure 7.32) controls the font used in Finder windows, and the size of the icons used when windows are displayed by name, date, kind, and so on (exceptions being, by icon and by small icon). You'll like this.

Views

Figure 7.32
Views control panel icon

1. Click on the Control Panels folder and view the contents by Name (**Views** menu).

2. Find and open the Views control panel (double-click).

3. Drag the Views control panel around so you can see the Control Panels window and the control panel at the same time. Resize the window if necessary.

It ought to look something like figure 7.33 when you're done.

GENIUS TIP

Whenever you see a little black triangle in a menu or dialog box, it means there is more stuff in whatever direction the triangle is pointing. To get to that stuff, put the tip of the pointer on the triangle and hold down the mouse button. Presto, there's more stuff for you to choose from.

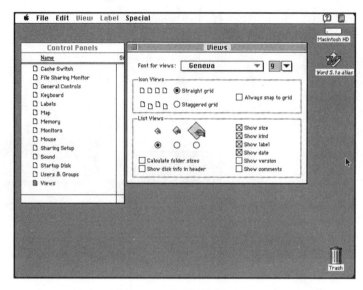

Figure 7.33
Views control panel and the Control Panels window viewed by Name

4. Choose a font and a size from the pop-up menus at the top of the control panel.

   Look at the Control Panels window. It changed! Figure 7.34 shows what I did—yours will probably be different.

5. Click on the mid-sized icon's button in the bottom left of the Views control panel. Look at the Control Panel window.

   It's changed again! The icons aren't so plain now—since they're bigger, there's a lot more detail (figure 7.35).

6. Play around until you've got things the way you like them, then close the Views control panel.

   You should be feeling pretty powerful now.

mAC LiNGO

The menus with the black triangles are called "pop-up" menus because they pop up when selected. What will they think of next?

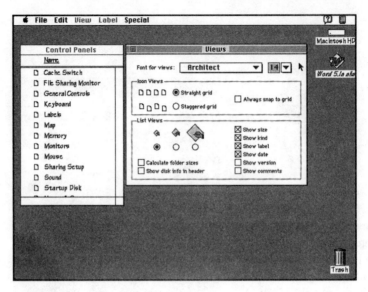

Figure 7.34
After adjusting font and size

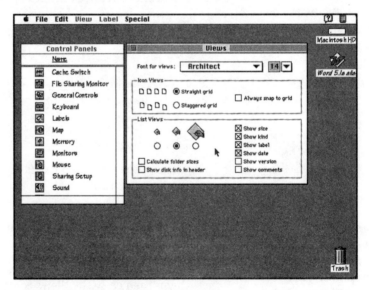

Figure 7.35
After adjusting icon sizes

Monitors

Color monitors are sometimes set, accidentally, to black and white. It wasn't very long ago that Apple itself was the guilty party. Knowing how to work the Monitors control panel will ensure that you can switch to color in an instant.

1. Open the Monitors control panel (figure 7.36). You'll see the controls in the open control panel (figure 7.37).

2. Assuming you have a color Mac (this is a waste of time if you don't), click on black and white in the Monitors control panel.

    Boring, eh?

3. Click on the highest number in the list.

    Yes, there are reasons for the numbers they give. Here's a hint: "Powers of 2." You're back to color.

4. Click on the Grays button.

    Presto, you're Ansel Adams.

5. Choose the settings you want (remember: more shades equals lower performance, and it doesn't matter whether you're looking at "colors" or "grays"). Close the Monitors control panel.

Monitors

Figure 7.36
Monitors control panel icon

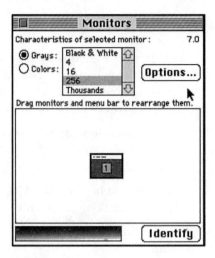

Figure 7.37
Monitors control panel

Why not switch to color and be done? Because Macs run fastest in black and white. It's easier for the Mac to display a black and white screen than a color one, and it takes less computer processing power. Sometimes you need all the power you can get (especially when you're working with large databases, large spread- sheets, or large anythings). Switching to black and white is the easiest way to jump a notch in perfor- mance.

General

This control panel has many personalities. You'll be amazed at what you can do with it. We'll try the tricky one: changing the Desktop pattern. The others you can explore on your own.

1. Find and open the General control panel (figure 7.38).

    You'll see what's pictured in figure 7.39.

General Controls

Figure 7.38
General control panel icon

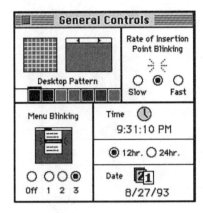

Figure 7.39
General control panel

2. The Desktop pattern (and color) is controlled by the area at the upper left of the General control panel. The square on the left is a zoomed-in view of the pattern on the right. If you click in the white area at the top of the pattern on the right, you'll cycle through the patterns and colors that Apple's provided for you. Figure 7.40 shows you where to click.

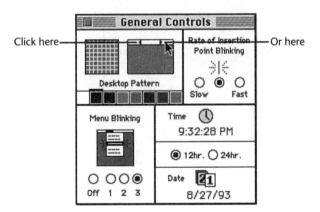

Figure 7.40
Where to click to cycle through patterns

3. When you find a pattern you like, click right on the pattern (in the box on the right). Figure 7.41 shows you where.

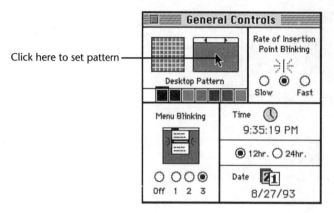

Click here to set pattern

Figure 7.41
Where to click to choose a pattern

If you don't like any of the preset patterns, you can make your own. Start by finding the closest thing to what you want. Then:

1. Click on a color, effectively "loading your brush." Figure 7.42 shows you where to choose a color.

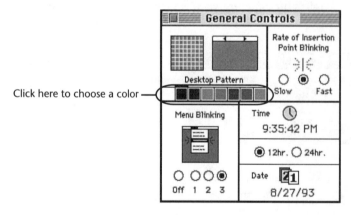

Click here to choose a color

Figure 7.42
Where to choose a color

2. Click in the zoomed-in pattern area (the square on the left).

   You'll leave behind a dot of the color you chose.

3. Continue to choose colors and make dots until you like what you've done.

The pattern will stay on the desktop through restarts and shut downs. However, if you cycle through to look at other patterns your creation will disappear. Naturally there's a way to avoid this problem: Just double-click in the same box you clicked in to apply the pattern to the Desktop. This puts your pattern into the loop, where it will stay.

4. Click once on the pattern in the box on the right (which is the actual-size view of the enlarged pattern on the left).

   This applies the pattern to the desktop.

5. When you're finished, close the General control panel.

It is probably pretty obvious to you that there are many, many control panels. Apple gives you a bunch, and you can buy a bunch more from third-party programmers. Whether "Apple standard" or not, each control panel does something to modify the way your Mac behaves.

Another folder, the Extensions folder (figure 7.43), holds items that are similar to control panels, except you can't control them. Extensions are either there or not there—you can't control them more than that. There's not much else to know, except that most Extensions are behind-the-scenes sorts of things (which may explain why you're not supposed to play with them).

Extensions

Figure 7.43
The Extensions folder

Startup Items Folder

n
o I'm not nuts for the
   Startup Items folder. I
t really don't have
   anything I want to
E open automatically at
   startup. If you do put
   things into it, keep the
   total number down to
   three or so.

You can force your address book (or any other application, document, and so on) to pop up when you start your Mac by putting an alias to the item into the Startup Items folder (figure 7.44). Actually, you could put the real items into the Startup Items folder, but the same reasoning used to convince you to use aliases in the Apple Menu Items folder goes for this one, too: leave things where they are, and fool around with aliases.

Startup Items

Figure 7.44
Startup Items

Fonts

Fonts used to be simple to understand. Hard to install, but simple to understand. Now it's the other way around. Thus, before telling you what you'll find in your System Folder, font-wise, I'll tell you generally how fonts work so you at least have some understanding of what's going on.

The most confusing issues in Macdom involve the proliferation and varying popularity of font standards. Currently, three font technologies compete: bitmapped, PostScript, and TrueType.

Bitmaps

They're called "bitmapped" because each piece of data is mapped onto the screen or paper bit by bit. And brother, that's a lot of bits!

Bitmapped fonts are collections of dots arranged to look like letters and numbers. The original Macintosh shipped with a handful of bitmapped fonts—not many by today's standards, but a veritable font cornucopia in 1984. The bitmap standard's strength was its simplicity: a single font file contained every-thing necessary for appearing in menus, displaying on screen, and printing on paper. The drawback of bitmaps is they scale horribly.

Figure 7.45 shows a 12-point bitmap scaled to 96-point. Notice how jagged it looks! It doesn't matter which way you scale a bitmap (up or down), it just doesn't look good. The only way out is to install every size of every bitmapped font you can get your hands on. This gets old very fast and also takes a lot of room on the hard disk.

nOtE *There are 72 points to an inch. This is typographer talk.*

Figure 7.45
12-point font scaled to 96-point

When PostScript laser printers were invented, some of the trouble with bitmaps went away. If you used the "right" fonts you'd get smooth output, no matter how lousy the screen looked. If you used other fonts you'd get lousy output, no matter what. It was and is confusing.

Enter PostScript fonts, stage left.

PostScript Fonts

note *PostScript is a programming language developed by Adobe Systems, Inc. Other companies make and sell PostScript fonts but they all use Adobe's technology.*

PostScript fonts aren't collections of dots like bitmaps are. PostScript fonts are collections of instructions that tell a printer how to construct each character. The instructions are a lot like high school algebra: Draw a straight line connecting these two points, then turn 37 degrees counterclockwise and continue in that direction for one inch, etc. Theoretical stuff.

The big advantage of PostScript fonts is their scalability: Since each character is really a set of mathematical instructions, scaling them is a piece of cake and it doesn't make them scruffy. Figure 7.46 shows a PostScript font scaled to 96-point. This smoothness at any size makes PostScript fonts a big hit with artists and designers and everyone else who cares how things look.

note *PostScript fonts don't come in sizes. There's no need for that, since a single font file contains instructions for scaling to any size. PostScript fonts typically have slightly funny names, such as "HelvBld" instead of bold Helvetica, a convention which appears to have been agreed upon over several pitchers of beer.*

M

Figure 7.46
PostScript font, scaled

The problem with PostScript fonts is they're only good for printing. You can't add a PostScript font to your word processor's font menu; you have to add a bitmap with the same name. You can't display a PostScript font on the screen; again, you have to use a bitmapped font. You can see how confusing this can be.

Recapping, we so far have a choice of using a bitmapped font for menus, the screen (probably looking scruffy), and printing (probably also looking scruffy), *or* a bitmapped font for menus, the same bitmapped font for the screen (probably scruffy), and a PostScript font for gorgeous printing (with an option to use ATM and the PostScript font for the screen as well). These are not great alternatives. Something had to be done.

That something was the invention of a third font "standard." This one, called TrueType, came from Apple.

Adobe Type Manager, or "ATM," in the jargon, lets you use PostScript fonts for displaying text on the screen. That's how I made figure 7.46 look so good. Look into ATM (it's cheap, but the PostScript fonts aren't) if nice-looking type is important to you.

TrueType Fonts

TrueType fonts provide a neat and tidy solution to the font problem. A TrueType font contains everything necessary to make the font appear in menus while simultaneously holding PostScript-like instructions that make text look great on screen and on the printed page.

TrueType fonts offer some other advantages, too. For one thing, they're free, or nearly so. Apple ships a bunch of them with every Mac they sell, and they ship a bunch more with each printer. For another, they don't depend on Adobe Type Manager to look good on screen. For a third, they're probably already installed on your Mac.

So why is it you never hear about TrueType, only about PostScript? That's an easy one: PostScript came first, and the world embraced it. TrueType showed up years later and being the new kid on the block has not been an advantage. Throw in the fact that TrueTypes don't print quite as well as PostScript fonts do and you get today's situation: a large installed base of PostScript font users (relatively long-term Mac folks, mostly) and a growing base of TrueType users (relative newcomers).

Which Fonts for You?

Determining which font technology you should use isn't very hard (though it sounds like it ought to be). The first question to ask yourself is, "Am I a graphic arts professional?" If you are, or think you are, or think you might want to be, go with the PostScript fonts and stay far, far away from TrueTypes. Despite Apple's propaganda, TrueType fonts are *not* completely compatible with PostScript fonts, and you'll have many strange problems if you try to mix things up. Service bureaus (places with million-dollar printers that charge you to print your work) use PostScript almost exclusively, and if you're going to be an artist, you'd better be compatible with your service bureau. Yes, you'll have to deal with strangely-named font files, and yes, you'll have to install ATM, and yes, you'll have a tougher time in general when it comes to installing fonts, but this is the price you pay for being an artist.

The second question to ask yourself (assuming you said, "No, I'm not a graphic artist") is, "Am I cheap?" If you are, or think you are, or think you might want to be, stick with the TrueTypes. They're easy to install, they look good no matter what, and their prices can't be beat.

Now, how to install the rascals.

How to Install Fonts

Okay, gang, listen up. This is where it gets weird. On the one hand, you need to know which system you're using because you need to know where your fonts should be installed. On the other hand, you don't need to know which system you're using because your Mac will put your fonts in the right place for you. I recommend you find out which system you're running so you'll know where to look for fonts should you someday want to remove some.

The first step in installing fonts is to find some fonts to install. Figure 7.47 shows the icons for a bitmapped, a PostScript, and a TrueType font—and a *font suitcase* which could hold one or several bitmapped and/or TrueType (but not PostScript) fonts. I told you this was confusing.

Figure 7.47
Font icons

The best way to install fonts is to drag them to your *closed* System Folder. If you do this, your Mac will (under System 7.1) move the fonts to a Fonts folder (figure 7.48), whether you drag bitmaps, PostScripts, TrueTypes, or suitcases. If you're using System 7.0 or 7.0.1 (more confusion!) your Mac will move everything but the PostScripts into the system file itself. The Mac moves the PostScripts to the Extensions folder.

Fonts

Figure 7.48
Fonts folder (system 7.1 only)

GENIUS TIP

This automatic font distribution only works when you drag fonts to a closed System Folder. Dragging fonts to an open System Folder might seem more sensible but you'll short-circuit things if you do it. Don't.

I hope you believe me that it's a lot easier to let the Mac do the work. Fonts won't work if they're not installed properly; if you're not sure where things go, drag them to your closed System Folder and let your Mac sort things out.

In closing this most technical of subjects, here are my five rules for happy font use. Your Mac and your printer will thank you for following them.

1. Never install TrueType and PostScript versions of the same font.

2. Never install more than two sizes of a bitmap if you have a corresponding TrueType version or a PostScript one with ATM.

3. Avoid installing TrueType versions of fonts that are built into your PostScript printer.

4. Avoid using (or even installing) TrueType fonts if you intend to print your work at a service bureau.

5. Periodically inspect your Fonts folder (if you have one) and your system file for stray fonts. Be sure you need everything that's installed—the fewer fonts you have, the faster your Mac will run.

That's it for fonts. Clearly, this is no simple subject—but you've got the basics now.

In Summary

The System Folder is where the "this is so easy" charade falls apart. Sorry to be the bearer of bad news, but that's the way it goes. I encourage you to poke around and explore—but please be careful doing it.

Naturally it's time for a quiz. I'll go easy on you; this is a tough chapter.

1. Do all Macs have a System Folder?

2. How many System Folders should your Mac have?

3. Do you know what an operating system is?

4. Do you know what the Finder does?

5. Can you pop out a folder's contents?

6. Are you convinced that aliases are wonderful?

7. Can you put items into the **Apple** menu?

8. Do you know how to use Key Caps?

9. Do you know how to use the Scrapbook? Do you know why it's cool?

10. Are you comfy with the items in the Control Panels folder?

11. Are Extensions modifiable?

12. What's the Startup Items folder?

13. Lucky thirteen. Can you identify TrueType, bitmapped, and PostScript fonts by their icons?

14. Aren't you glad this chapter's over?

Chapter 8
Routine Procedures

There exists in this world a fortuitous balancing system that keeps our Planet from careening into the Void. Examples abound:

- Yin and Yang
- Girls and Boys
- Peanut Butter and Jelly
- Field & Stream

The Macintosh provides further proof of this principle. Amazingly, every second you save by using a Mac is handed back to the Time Gods as you perform the routine but necessary procedures that keep your Mac alive. Incredibly, the boredom you'll experience while performing these procedures is *precisely* equal to the terror you'll someday experience if you *don't* perform them. You can't win. So why do any maintenance at all?

Good question. Equally good answer (see? yet another example of balance): for the money. Not the money it costs for the programs. I'm talking about the value of the work you've created and stored on your Mac. "Priceless" may be overdoing it, but not by much. Take my advice: don't take chances. The cost when you lose is too much.

Backing Up

Backing up means making extra copies of your work and storing them somewhere safe. "Somewhere safe" means on disks or tapes, away from your Mac, and away from the usual baddies of fire, flood, direct sunlight, and cats. This way, if something happens to your Mac (heck, even if someone swipes it), you won't lose all your work.

Backing up can be as simple and straightforward as dragging everything on your hard disk onto floppy disks, then storing the disks in a drawer. You can buy special *backup programs* that help with this procedure, and often this is the best way to go. Anything that makes backing up less of a chore (and therefore something you're more likely to do) is something worth considering. Especially considering that these programs typically cost less than one hundred bucks.

Cleaning Up the Software

One of the nice things about backing up your work is that you don't have to worry (well, not too much, anyway) about throwing away the wrong thing when you decide to clean up. It's a good idea to take a good look at your Mac's hard disk every couple of weeks and toss the things you don't need. You'll save space and you might make your Mac work better to boot.

Most importantly, look through your System Folder. You've already learned about the importance of the control panels, extensions, and the Apple menu items folders; now is the time to look inside the system folder for stuff that just isn't necessary.

How do you know what isn't necessary? That's a good question. Start by looking for control panels, extensions, and Apple menu items that don't apply to your Mac. For instance, if your Mac isn't a PowerBook, items called "Portable," "Battery," and "PowerBook Display" aren't going to help you. If you don't have a modem, files such as "Communications Toolbox," "Modem Tool," and the like aren't going to help you, either. These files have a way of appearing seemingly by themselves (though the truth is that someone, once upon a time, actually installed them for you, probably meaning you no harm.

Just be careful of the really, really important files (figure 8.1), or you could have a very, very bad day.

System   Finder   System Enabler 040

Figure 8.1
Really, really important files: System, Finder, and System Enabler files

You don't have to really throw things away to clean up. Just move them to a "holding tank" and leave them there a while. When I clean up, I move questionable items to a folder called "Toss these 7/27/94" or something similar. I generally make the date a week or two away. On that date, if my Mac is running well and I haven't missed the questionable items, I drop them into the Trash and empty it. This idea works very well; you should try it.

Cleaning Up the Hardware

This isn't a big concern, but you'll occasionally want to clean the outside of your Mac as well. Monitors get dusty, keyboards get greasy, mice get yucky. Here's how to take care of them.

Cleaning the Monitor

The only things to worry about here are scratching the glass and causing an explosion. The scratching problem is eliminated by using the famous "soft, lint-free cloth" you've probably read about. Explosions are prevented by spraying the glass cleaner onto the cloth, not on the screen, and by doing the cleaning with the Mac and the monitor turned off. It's far-fetched, but there is a chance that liquid could get around the glass and into the monitor itself if you squirt it directly on the glass; the next time the power is turned on, the liquid could cause a short circuit, an explosion, and a bunch of other problems after that. Just be reasonably careful and everything will be fine.

Cleaning the Keyboard

Keyboard keys get greasy from being touched billions of times. You can use the same soft, lint-free cloth you used for the monitor to wipe down the keys; again, be smart and squirt the cleaner onto the cloth, not on the keyboard itself.

That was easy.

Cleaning the Mouse

A dirty mouse makes moving the cursor very awkward.
Sometimes the cursor will jump, sometimes it will skip, sometimes it will work perfectly, and sometimes it won't work at all.
Cleaning the mouse isn't as easy as cleaning the screen, but
it's worth it. Do this when your cursor won't do what your
mouse tells it to.

1. Turn your mouse on its back.

2. Loosen the ring surrounding the mouse ball (you need to
   loosen it so you can get the ball out). New-ish mice have a
   ring that spins. Old-ish mice have a ring that slides.

3. Remove the ring, then remove the ball (if you turn the
   mouse right-side-up the ball will simply fall out).

4. Wipe the ball off with that soft, lint-free cloth.

5. Look inside the mouse, where the ball used to be. See
   those little rollers? You need to clean them. Use a tooth-
   pick or a fingernail to scrape the gook off of them. Be sure
   to spin the rollers all the way around—if you only clean
   half the roller, you'll only make things worse.

6. Put the ball back into the hole.

7. Put the ring back on and tighten it up by spinning or
   sliding as appropriate.

You can check your owner's manual for more inside dirt on
getting the inside dirt out of the mouse.

Hard Disk Maintenance

Oh boy. I'll bet you've already heard people talk about
"defragmenting" and "rebuilding" and "optimizing" your hard
disk. I'll bet they've convinced you that your hard disk will stop
working if you don't pay attention to these and other critical
operations.

Baloney.

The fact is, you can get along fine without any of that. With
any luck at all, your disk will keep a-working all by itself (of
course, you've got your backups just in case, right?).

In all fairness, it's not a bad idea to defragment, rebuild, and optimize your hard disk, but you'll probably notice little if any improvement. Here for your edification, though, is how these things are done.

Defragmenting

Remember in *The Wizard of Oz* when the winged monkeys threw pieces of Scarecrow every which way? His arms were over *here*, his legs were over *there*. Believe it or not, your files are stored on your hard disk in a very similar manner.

It works this way: Suppose you have a brand-new empty hard disk and you want to store a two-page letter on it. No problem: your Mac lays it down, right at the beginning of the disk (figure 8.2). Now suppose you write a second letter and you want to store it, too. Your Mac lays the second letter down right after the first, neat as you please (figure 8.3). Which naturally leads to a problem—namely, what happens when you add a couple of pages to the first letter? If you said, "It pushes the second letter down the road a piece," you're wrong. (Good idea, but wrong. See how unintuitive this whole computer business is?)

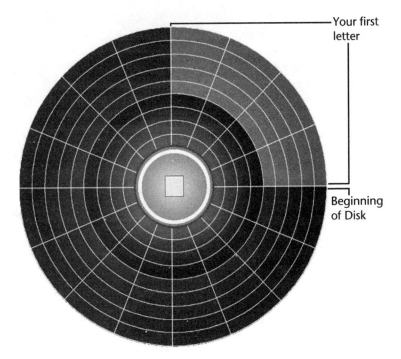

Figure 8.2
First letter on disk

What really happens is that the new pages for the first letter are stored after the old pages of the second letter (figure 8.4). Thus, the first letter isn't all in one piece. It's *fragmented*. Fragmented documents can't be read from the disk in a single pass since they're not in a single piece; the time spent looking for all the pieces slows your Mac down.

Defragmenting is the process by which your files are rearranged on the hard disk to eliminate fragmentation. In our two-letter example, the second letter would be moved past the new pages of the first letter. Then the new pages of the first letter would be moved to eliminate the gap between them and the rest of the first letter (figure 8.5). You'd use a defragmenting program to make this work.

"Fragmented" means separated into fragments. Fragments are pieces. So a fragmented file is one that is separated into pieces. That's logical, right?

"Defragmenting" is the reverse and so is un-separating the pieces. Thus, defragmenting is the process of joining all the pieces together again into one continuous block of data. You see, it's not really that complicated; it's just the big, scary sounding words that are intimidating.

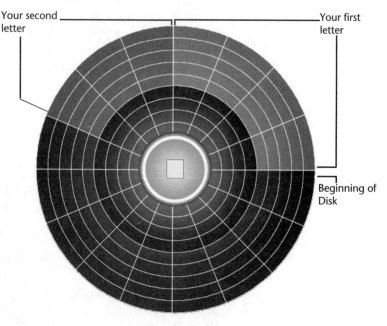

Your second letter ──────── Your first letter

Beginning of Disk

Figure 8.3
Second letter on disk

Depending on the program, the second letter might be moved to eliminate the gap between it and the first letter (figure 8.6). If it is moved, you can see that adding a page to the first letter will lead to fragmentation again (figure 8.7).

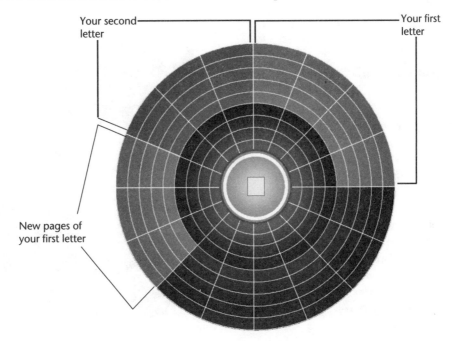

Your second letter

Your first letter

New pages of your first letter

Figure 8.4
Storing the new pages of your first letter

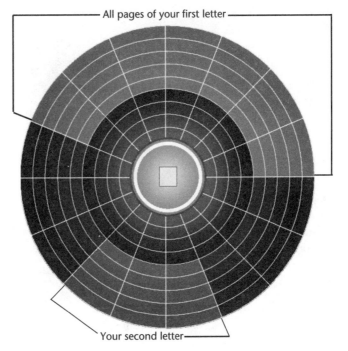

All pages of your first letter

Your second letter

Figure 8.5
Moving the second letter and joining the parts of your first letter

Some programs do more than unite the pieces of your files. They arrange your files on the hard disk in a sensible pattern: System Folder here, applications there, documents somewhere else. This procedure is called optimizing the disk. Some people mistakenly call routine defragmenting "optimizing." They shouldn't; the procedures are not equivalent. Optimizers defragment files, then arrange them in groups. Defragmenters simply defragment.

As usual, there are exceptions to the rule. If you regularly work with graphics files that are bigger than a couple of megabytes, each defragmenting might make a noticeable difference.

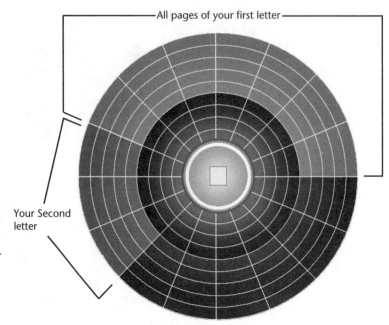

Figure 8.6
After moving the second letter

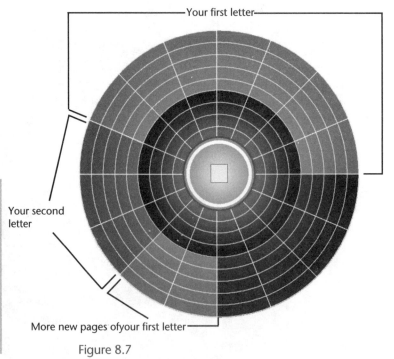

Figure 8.7
Fragmented again

Naturally, the real question is, "Should you worry about it?" I say, "No." First of all, the performance difference between a fragmented hard disk and the same disk after defragmenting is very, very slight. I doubt that you'd notice. Second of all, defragmenting a hard disk means moving every file around, which not only takes time, but is a bit of a risk (if the power goes out while you're defragmenting you're not going to like what happens). Personally, I don't think it's worth the trouble.

Rebuilding the Desktop File

Surely you've noticed that the Mac knows which icon goes with which file. Word processing documents get word processing icons, folders get folder icons, control panels get control panel icons, and so on. Figure 8.8 shows some of these.

A Word document   A folder   Monitors   Memory

Figure 8.8
Good, descriptive icons

You also may have noticed that files occasionally lose their icons. Instead of good, descriptive icons, such as those shown in figure 8.8, you sometimes see bad, generic icons, like the ones shown in figure 8.9. If you see any icons like those, it's time to rebuild the desktop file.

Joe Bland   Mr. Generic   No Personality

Figure 8.9
Bad, generic icons

The desktop file keeps track of which icon goes with which file, and sometimes the desktop file goes bad. Not exactly confidence-inspiring, but that's the way it is. Rebuilding the desktop file is a piece of cake, though. Just restart your Mac and hold the Command and Option keys down while it is restarting. You'll see a message asking you if you really want to rebuild (figure 8.10); you do.

GENIUS TIP

Rebuilding the desktop file does more than pretty up the icons. It re-links files back to the programs that created them. If, for example, the icon on a Word document goes bad, that document won't open when you double-click on it. After rebuilding the desktop file and getting the icons back in gear, the double-click will work.

Rebuilding the desktop file will take a few minutes, but there's no need to watch. Stick around long enough to be sure it's started rebuilding, then break for coffee. When the desktop file is completely rebuilt, your icons will be good as new.

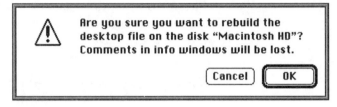

⚠ **Are you sure you want to rebuild the desktop file on the disk "Macintosh HD"? Comments in info windows will be lost.**

Cancel   OK

Figure 8.10
Rebuilding the desktop file

Rebuilding the desktop file is so simple and so good that I recommend you do it every time you think about it. Once each month isn't too often. And, when you're having troubles, a quick desktop file rebuild is sometimes the easiest cure.

Installing Software

This isn't exactly maintenance, but it's important stuff anyhow. Here's how to install your software so it works right from the start.

note
You may be wondering where this desktop file is stored. It's on the hard disk, but it's invisible. This is an important file, and the Mac doesn't want you monkeying with it (except when you rebuild, which is a very controlled procedure). Many of the files that do the dirty work on a Mac are invisible (which simply means they don't get icons). There's more going on behind the scenes than you think.

- Read the directions. You'd be amazed at how well this can work. Sometimes programs tell you how to customize an installation to include only those parts important to you. You might not want, for example, to install the voice annotation files in Microsoft Word 5.1. If you read the directions, you'll find out how to skip them.

- Read the directions again.

- Back up your stuff before installing anything new. This is particularly important when updating old programs, since the installation procedure may erase the previous version of the software.

n **o** **t** **E** *It doesn't matter which Shift key you use. It also doesn't matter if you hold a Shift key down while choosing Restart from the Special menu. By the way, you can let go as soon as you see the "Extensions Off" message.*

- Before installing new software, restart your Mac with the Shift key held down. This turns off every system enhancement you have, including file sharing, clocks, screen savers, and so on. What's left is just plain Mac, which is better for the installation procedure. If you don't see a message saying "Extensions Off," something went wrong. Try it again, but be quicker with the Shift key.

- Use the Installer, if there is one. Practically every program that comes on more than one disk includes an Installer on a disk called "Disk 1" (or something equally imaginative). Software companies usually include Installers because they think their programs are difficult to install otherwise. They're probably right. USE THE INSTALLER.

- Restart your Mac after installing any software.

- Try your new software. If it works, wonderful. If not, call the company that made it and have them walk you through a reinstallation. You'll find a Technical Support phone number in most manuals.

n **o** **t** **E** *By the way, it still counts as "stealing" even if your friend "gives" you the software. It's the software manufacturer that gets hurt.*

Needless to say—but what the heck—it's a bad idea to copy software from friends and stick it on your hard disk. Many programs come in more than one piece, which means you either need an Installer, the original disks, the manual, or maybe all three. Hardly a week goes by without someone telling me that they got such-and-such a program from a friend and it doesn't work. The reason, nine out of ten times, is they didn't get all the pieces. As if stealing software isn't bad enough... these people don't even steal it correctly. Sheesh.

If you follow this chapter's guidelines you'll save time, tears, and money. The next chapter offers help when, in spite of your following these routine procedures religiously, your Mac acts up. But first, the Quiz.

1. Are you convinced that you ought to back up your work?

2. Do you know which kind of floppy disks to use for backups?

3. Do you know how to clean your monitor?

4. Do you know how to clean your mouse, and do you know how to tell when it's time to do it?

5. Do you understand why defragmenting is risky and often a waste of time?

6. Do you understand the value of rebuilding your desktop file?

7. Do you know how to rebuild your desktop file?

8. Do you know how to install new software?

9. Would you like fries with that?

Chapter 9
Trouble Shooting

You'd think a computer would be more than reliable. You'd think it would be downright solid. Consistent. Predictable.

You'd be wrong.

Macs don't always behave the way we want them to. Sometimes the Mac is to blame; it's possible (though not likely) that the Mac is simply defective. Sometimes the Mac's design is to blame; Apple has put out some Mac models that weren't quite ready for prime time. Most often, it's the software we put on our Macs that's to blame; it could be our fault, for installing it wrong, or it could be the programmer's fault, for writing a buggy program.

Knowing who to blame is nice, partly because it makes us feel better, but mostly because it helps us know how to solve the problems. This chapter teaches you how to solve the problems you can solve and how to recognize the problems you cannot.

Bombs Away

Far and away the most common Mac problem is the *system error* (figure 9.1).

Figure 9.1
System error dialog box

Generally speaking, a bomb (sometimes called a *system crash*, or just a *crash*) is the result of a programming error. And, generally speaking, there's nothing you can do about it, except to try in future to avoid doing whatever it was you were doing when you bombed.

Always assume that a system error is caused by software. Ninety-nine out of one hundred times, you'll be right (and the one time you're wrong you can't fix the problem yourself anyway). The problem could be caused by one bad program, but it's usually the interaction *between* programs that brings out the worst. The more complicated your setup, the more interactions, and the more you're going to crash. Consider this: Your Mac is always running the Finder; it's always running the System; it's probably running several extensions and control panels (remember, things such as screen savers, reminders, and clocks are *always* running, from the instant your Mac starts up to when you turn it off—or crash); and it may be running one or more programs such as Word or Excel.

Follow these steps to solve your crashing problems:

1. Restart your Mac with the Shift key down.

   This turns off all extensions, which means things such as screen savers, reminders, and clocks won't start up, making your Mac more pristine and generally easier for programs to get along with. You'll get a message like the one shown in figure 9.2 if you're doing it right. Don't let go of the Shift key until you've seen the message.

Figure 9.2
Extensions off message

note There's an old joke about a fellow who tells his doctor, "It hurts when I do this." The doctor replies, "Don't do that." It's pretty much the same with system errors. Something you did caused a program to go nuts. You'll solve the problem by not doing that again. The hard part is figuring out what you did.

note Remember, extensions start running when you start up your Mac. There's no way to turn them off without restarting. Holding the Shift key down during a restart prevents extensions from loading, period. Restarting without the Shift key held down allows every extension in the Extensions folder, Control Panels folder, or loose in the System Folder to start up.

n
o *Very sorry to report*
t *that an extension*
E *problem does not*
necessarily mean that
the problem has
anything to do with
something in the
Extensions folder.
Control Panels are also
extensions, in many
cases, and they may be
the source of your
problem.

2. Try doing what you were doing when your Mac bombed.

   If it doesn't bomb, you've identified the problem as an extension problem. That means you'll need to figure out exactly which one causes the trouble, which means lots of trial and error, not to mention lots of restarting.

   Use steps 3-7 below. If it still bombs, skip steps 3-7 and then continue reading.

3. Open the Extensions folder (it's in the System Folder) and take everything out of it. Put the contents on the Desktop (next to the Trash). Restart (without holding down the Shift key).

4. Try doing what you were doing when your Mac bombed.

   If it doesn't bomb, you've reduced the problem to something from the Extensions folder.

5. Move about half of the extensions back into the Extensions folder. Restart (without holding down the Shift key).

6. Try doing what you were doing when your Mac bombed.

   If it doesn't bomb, you've reduced the problem to one of the remaining extensions. Add them a few at a time to the Extensions folder, restarting and trying to make your Mac crash. When it finally does, you've found your culprit.

   If removing extensions from the Extensions folder didn't solve your problem, the problem's probably in the Control Panels folder. Remove its contents as you did for the Extensions folder and restart. Repeat the drill above until you've found the guilty Control Panel.

7. Call the company that made the bad extension/control panel and describe your problem. You might learn of a new version of the extension/control panel; you might learn of a new version of *another* extension or control panel.

If your extensions and control panels are up to date but you're still crashing like mad, a single hope remains. Remember, your extensions and control panels load alphabetically: you can rename them to rearrange them, and that may solve the problem. Assuming you know which extension or control panel is to blame, try putting a space in front of its name to make it load sooner, or a "z" in front of its name to make it load later. Restart and see how it goes.

nOtE *This business of removing files from the Extensions and Control Panels folders is a real drag (pun intended). So is rearranging the extension loading order by renaming the things. Luckily, a class of programs called "extension managers" makes these jobs much simpler. I use the Startup Manager from the Now Utilities package (see Chapter 5), but several others exist. Get and use an extension manager if you've got more than five icons hopping across your screen at startup.*

nOtE *Preference files store personalized settings. Trashing a preference file means your program will look the way it did right out of the box: generic as anything, without any of your personalized settings. You'll have to spend some time resetting those preferences, but it's a small price to pay for getting your program to work.*

Naturally, it's possible that your problem isn't caused by bad extensions or control panels. You might have a bad program, or a bad copy of a good program. Sometimes you can look like a genius by solving the problem this way:

1. Look for a folder called "Preferences" in the System Folder. Open it.

2. Look for a file called "MyProgram Prefs" or "MyProgram Settings" or "MyProgram *anything*" where "MyProgram" is the name of the program that's not working properly. If you find such a file, you're almost done (if you can't find such a file, you're out of luck).

3. Move the file from the Preferences folder to the Desktop, next to the Trash.

4. Restart your Mac and try your program again. If it works, toss the old file into the Trash and forget about it. You're done.

Started with Extensions off, trashed the preference file, and still no luck? Try reinstalling the program from original master disks. Still no luck? You're running out of options, but here they are:

- Call the company that made your program and describe your problem. Sometimes they can solve your problems by sending you a new version of the program (and usually it's not a version they advertise, so you've got to ask).

- Reinstall your system software from original master disks.

- Learn to live without the program.

No Printing

If it isn't a system error that's getting to you, it's probably a printing problem. (Sometimes it's a system error that appears when you print—a double whammy). Here's how to solve this problem:

1. Turn your printer off. Wait a while (I wait long enough to get a fresh cup of coffee).

2. Check the cabling. Printers are usually, but not always, connected to Macs via printer ports. Look on the back of your Macintosh to see which port the printer cable's

connected to; the one with the picture of a printer is the printer port. The one with the picture of a phone is the modem port.

3. Turn the printer on and wait for it to warm up.

   You'll know it's warmed up when the lights on the printer aren't flashing. (If it's not a laser printer, it will warm up immediately. Laser printers take a couple of minutes.)

4. Choose the **Chooser** from the **Apple** menu.

5. Click once on the icon that represents your printer. Figure 9.3 shows a Chooser window with icons for some printers, your actual icon may vary.

They call it the Chooser because it lets you choose a network service. In this case, you're choosing a service called "printing." The Chooser was a good idea once but it's sort of a drag today. I'd bet on the Chooser disappearing in a couple of years.

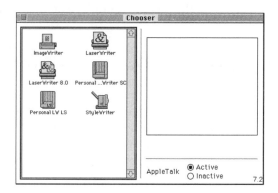

Figure 9.3
The Chooser

n
o **You probably want to**
t **throw away the**
E **printer icons for**
printers you don't
have. Look in the
Extensions folder inside
the System Folder; that's
where they are.

6. Clicking on the printer icon should have produced something in the right-hand side of the Chooser. If you've got a PostScript laser printer, you'll see a message saying "Please select a PostScript laser printer." If you've got an ImageWriter, or any other non-PostScript device, you'll get a message saying "Please select a port."

7. If you have a PostScript laser printer, do what the message says and click on the name of the laser writer you want to use. If you have a non-PostScript printer, choose the port corresponding to the place your printer's plugged into.

8. Close the Chooser and try printing again. If it works, terrific. Otherwise, continue with Step 9.

9. Make a new document and try printing it. If it works, suspect that your problem document is probably bad. If it doesn't work, go to step 10.

10. Try printing something created with another program. That is, if you're having trouble printing a Word document, try printing an Excel document. If it works, your other program is probably bad. Reinstall the program and try again.

11. If you're still having trouble, reinstall the printing software from original disks.

12. Still having trouble? Restart with the Shift key down. If you can print now, you've got an extension problems; see the section "Bombs Away" for advice.

Damaged Hard Drive

Disappearing files, files that won't save, and generally odd behavior are signs of a damaged hard drive. Fix the problems with Norton Utilities, MacTools, Safe & Sound, or Disk First Aid (the first three are commercial software, the last one comes with your Mac). I like Safe & Sound the best.

Run Safe & Sound (or whatever you end up using) over and over until it reports no problems. Then, assuming your disk is fixed, copy your important files onto floppy disks so that you've got some insurance. I make backups every night. So should you.

Damaged Floppy Disks

Sometimes you'll insert a floppy disk and get a message like the one shown in figure 9.4.

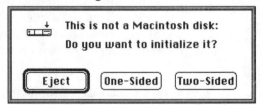

Figure 9.4
This disk is damaged

You're supposed to get this message with blank disks, but not with disks you've used. If you do get this message, eject the disk immediately. Remember this: "initializing" is a nice way of saying "erasing." You'll be very sorry if you initialize a disk with good stuff on it.

Try reinserting the disk with the Command and Option keys held down. This forces the Mac to rebuild the desktop file (see chapter 8 for more on this), and often solves the problem.

Sometimes a disk goes bad because its shutter (the metal thing at one end of the disk) gets stuck. Try to slide it back and forth a couple of times. Then reinsert the disk and hope.

Still no good? Try spinning the spindle on the disk (look at its underside) a couple of degrees. A quarter turn is about right. Reinsert with fingers crossed. No?

Time for heavy artillery. Try running Norton Disk Doctor, MacTools, Safe and Sound, or Disk First Aid on the disk. With luck, you'll be able to repair the disk; even without luck, you'll probably be able to copy stuff off the disk and move it to your hard disk.

Regardless of how you rescue your disk, copy everything on it to your hard disk immediately. Then eject the floppy and turn it into a coaster. Never ever use that disk again. Disks cost only a buck each; this is not the place to be cheap.

GENIUS TIP

If restarting doesn't eject the disk, try restarting with your mouse button held down. This tells the Mac to eject the disk. No one knows this except us.

Floppy Disk Stuck in the Floppy Drive

Disks sometimes refuse to eject the way they're supposed to. Restarting will generally solve the problem, assuming the drive is functioning properly.

At last resort, straighten a large paper clip and stick it into the small hole to the right of the floppy drive opening. Press firmly, straight in. This ought to do it.

Icons Gone Generic

You're working away, minding your own business, when all of a sudden you notice some strange generic icons. Figure 9.5 shows some examples. The fix is easy (though figuring out the cause is tough): restart with the Command and Option keys held down. This will rebuild the desktop. When you do it, you'll get a message like figure 9.6; click on OK.

Joe Bland   Mr. Generic   No Personality

Figure 9.5
Generic icons

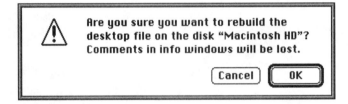

⚠ **Are you sure you want to rebuild the desktop file on the disk "Macintosh HD"? Comments in info windows will be lost.**

[Cancel]   [OK]

Figure 9.6
Rebuild the desktop? You betcha

If your icons still look bad, try running Norton or MacTools (see the "Damaged Hard Disk" section). Rebuild the desktop again. (For more information on rebuilding the desktop, see chapter 8.)

Disk is Full

This problem has three solutions:

- Throw things away until you have more room on the disk.

- Buy a bigger disk.

- Buy a compressing program such as AutoDoubler or Now Compress to squish your files down. I use Now Compress, but AutoDoubler is a close second.

note *Hard disks come in two flavors: internal and external. Internal disks fit inside your Mac and you never see them. External disks come in a little box and connect to your Mac with cables. It's generally easier to expand with an external disk since you get to leave the existing disk inside. On the other hand, external disks take up room on the desk. I have some of both... mostly because I didn't buy a big enough internal disk in the first place.*

GENIUS TIP

You can never have too much hard disk space. When it comes to buying hard drives, remember: More is better. Unfortunately, more is also more expensive. Buy the largest you can afford.

Compressing programs (such as AutoDoubler and Now Compress) are like pennies from heaven. They really work. They work by storing your files more efficiently than the Mac ordinarily would. Considering that they cost less than $100, and that hard disks cost a whole lot more than that, compression programs are terrific bargains. My out-of-space routine: first I throw stuff away. Then I compress. Then I throw away some more stuff. Finally, when I'm at the end of the line, I spend money and buy a new disk.

Not Enough Memory

It's extremely important to realize that this message (figure 9.7) does not refer to hard disk space. Most likely, you've got plenty of hard disk space; throwing things away isn't going to help.

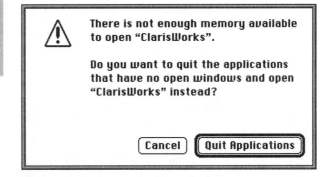

Figure 9.7
Out of memory message

Your problem involves RAM, which stands for Random Access Memory. Simply, this is your Mac's working memory, and it's typically much, much smaller than the permanent memory that your hard disk provides. Every program that's currently running (and *only* the running programs) uses RAM. Your job is to free some up. I'll show you how in a minute. First, let's be sure you know what RAM is.

Your hard disk is like a closet: it stores stuff until you're ready to use it. Even more like a closet, your hard disk stores more stuff than you (or your Mac) can handle at one time for example, you can't wear all your shoes at once; neither can your Mac run all your programs at once. If you could buy more feet, you could wear more shoes at once; similarly, if you could buy more RAM, you could run more programs at once. It happens that buying RAM is easier than buying feet (not to mention easier to install), but otherwise the analogy holds: RAM is like feet, your hard disk is like a closet, and your software is like shoes.

Wonder what's using your RAM? Click on your hard disk, then choose **About this Macintosh** from the **Apple** menu. You'll get something like figure 9.8 (but not exactly, since your Mac and my Mac aren't the same).

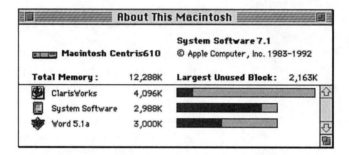

Figure 9.8
About this Macintosh

The bottom half of figure 9.8 shows where the RAM is going. Notice also the "Largest Unused Block." This is an important number. Here's why:

Every program needs RAM to run. When you double-click on a program, it has to fit into the largest unused block of RAM. Word 5.1 needs two megabytes (2,048K); Excel needs four megabytes. If your largest unused block of RAM isn't at least 2,048K, you can't run Word, and if it isn't at least 4,096K, you can't run Excel.

RAM is in use the minute you start a program and is released (for use by another program) the minute you quit that program. Important: *you have to Quit.* Closing windows is not the same thing. Let's experiment:

1. Restart your Mac by choosing **Restart** from the **Special** menu.

2. Look at the application menu to be sure only the Finder is running. Figure 9.9 shows what you should see; figure 9.10 shows what you shouldn't see. (If you see something like figure 9.10, quit each program until only the Finder is running.)

Figure 9.9
Application menu, Finder only

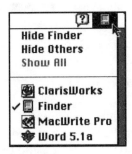

Figure 9.10
Application menu, Finder and everything else

3. Choose **About this Macintosh** from the **Apple** menu. Figure 9.11 shows how it might look. Jot down the number next to "Largest Unused Block." Leave the window open.

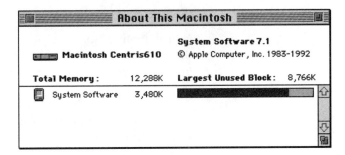

Figure 9.11
Before launching an application

4. Launch any application you wish. Just pick one and double-click.

5. Choose **Finder** from the Application menu.

6. Click on the "About this Macintosh" window again (or, if you can't see it, choose **About this Macintosh** from the **Apple** menu).

GENIUS TIP

*The System Software
includes the System, the
Finder, the fonts, the
extensions and the control
panels. This stuff loads
when you start your Mac,
and you can't quit any of
it. Thus, the System
Software is always taking
up RAM, and there's
nothing you can do about
it except run a leaner
system—one with fewer
fonts, fewer extensions, and
fewer control panels.*

Notice anything? You should; figure 9.12 shows what I saw.

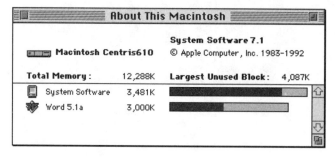

Figure 9.12
After opening a program

Notice in figure 9.12 that the program I'm running (Microsoft Word) has reserved 3,000K of RAM for itself. Notice also that it isn't using that much (the dark area represents the amount actually used while the light area represents how much is reserved). Finally, notice that the largest remaining block of RAM is smaller than it was before.

7. Go to the **Application** menu and choose the program that you launched in step 4.

8. Click on the close box.

   Notice the tiny icon atop the **Application** menu is still the icon of the program you launched. Know why? *Because the program is still running.*

9. Click on the "About this Macintosh" window again.

   Notice anything different? You shouldn't; your program is still running, still reserving RAM, and still making that smallest unused block smaller.

10. Use the **Application** menu to switch back to your program. Choose **Quit** from the **File** menu (heck, by now you oughta be doing Command-Q). Now look at the "About this Macintosh" window. It looks like it did when you started.

note *This is the key part of the exercise, so pay attention! If you're simply reading along and not doing it hands-on, be sure you read this part. Big, important stuff here!*

Here, then, is the Crucial Thing: closing the window isn't the same as quitting the program. Quitting puts the RAM back. Closing doesn't. Had you tried to launch a program that needed more RAM than the largest unused block, the Mac would have given you a message like figure 9.13.

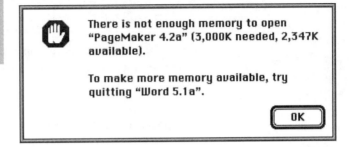

There is not enough memory to open "PageMaker 4.2a" (3,000K needed, 2,347K available).

To make more memory available, try quitting "Word 5.1a".

OK

Figure 9.13
Not enough memory

All this, and still you don't know how to avoid the "out of memory" messages. That's what you think. I think you know plenty. First, you know that the message refers to the program wanting more memory than the largest unused block. Second, you know that quitting programs puts RAM back, increasing the size of the largest unused block. Pretty straightforward: keep quitting programs until the largest unused block is big enough.

My Mac Seems Slow

Sometimes you'd swear your Mac is running half-speed. Opening folders takes forever, opening programs takes forever, saving takes forever, and printing takes forever. For some strange reason, this usually happens when you need the speed the most.

A slow Mac can often be sped up using one more of these techniques:

1. Restart your Mac (and restart your printer, if you're having printing troubles, too).

2. Reduce the number of items displayed in Finder windows. That means use lots of folders, and don't leave them popped out. Aim for fewer than 15 items per window.

note *A window with 15 folders in it, each with 1000 items, only knows about the 15 folders. This is a feature, not a bug; the Mac only keeps track of the things it can see, which speeds up everything. Remember: "more folders" is better.*

note *There's no speed advantage in displaying 256 grays instead of 256 colors. Speeds are identical regardless. Of course, going with grays makes you feel like Ansel Adams, and that's not bad.*

3. Use the Monitors control panel to reduce the number of shades displayed. Fewer shades means higher speed. A good compromise is 256 shades; if that's too slow, try 16.

4. Turn off every control panel that involves any sort of timer, then restart. This includes clocks, alarms, screen savers, and even—gasp—the Talking Moose (see Chapter 5). Personally, I'd leave the Moose and sacrifice a little speed, but the fact is that anything that watches your Mac's internal clock is siphoning off computing power, and the more of these gizmos you've got, the slower things will go.

5. Turn off every control panel that watches what you type, then restart. This includes spelling checkers that check what you type as you type it, and macro programs such as QuicKeys that want to do something when you press certain keys. These gizmos soak up computing power just like the timers do.

That's about all the "you can fix them" problems. Here now are some problems that *can* be fixed, but not by you (or me). These are called "take-your-wallet-and-your-Mac-to-the-Apple-Dealer" problems. Also in this section: some problems that can't be fixed at all; these are called "leave-the-Mac-at-home-but-don't-forget-your-wallet" problems.

The Mac Won't Start At All

If your Mac is deader than dead, without so much as a "bing" or a flashing light, it's looking pretty grim. Try these steps before giving up hope:

1. Disconnect everything from the Mac except the power cord and the monitor. This means printer cables, keyboard cables, mouse cables—everything. Naturally, you'll do this with the power off.

2. Be absolutely certain that you're plugging into an outlet that really works. Use a lamp to test the outlet; any old lamp will serve. So will a power drill. So will an electric train. (I don't care if you plug in a microwave oven and a set of hot rollers—just be sure the outlet works.)

3. Switch the Mac on, using the power switch on its case (remember, the keyboard's not attached anymore, so pressing the keyboard's power button won't do a thing).

Did it work? Cool. Your problem's probably not with the Mac itself. Most likely you've got a bad cable connecting the keyboard to the Mac. Either that or a bad keyboard. Regardless, there's nothing you can do except pay someone to repair or replace the defective component.

If you followed steps 1, 2, and 3, but your Mac still won't start, bring the whole thing (monitor, keyboard, mouse, and Mac) to a shop. Bring your receipt if the Mac is still under warranty.

GENIUS TIP

Remember: your Mac has a one-year warranty, and you can take your Mac to any Apple dealer for service. If your Mac's got a problem, they will fix it for free.

The Mac Starts, but There's a Sad Face on It

A sad-faced Mac (figure 9.14) means there's something really wrong. Sometimes you can fix this by disconnecting external devices such as scanners and hard drives, but often you can't. If you see a sad Mac at startup, turn it off, disconnect everything, and try again. If this doesn't do it, bring the whole setup to a shop.

Figure 9.14
Sad Mac

The Mac Starts, but There's a Floppy Disk Symbol with a Flashing Question Mark

Well, well, well. You're in a jam.

The blinking question mark means the Mac can't find a good System Folder on a good disk to start from. There's no way to know beforehand whether it's a bad System Folder on a good disk (trouble), a good System Folder on a bad disk (serious trouble), or a bad System Folder on a bad disk (yikes). If you've got Norton Utilities, MacTools, or Safe & Sound, now is the time to break it out and save the day. Each of these programs comes with some sort of emergency disk; stick that disk into the floppy drive and see what happens.

Norton, MacTools, and Safe & Sound can't do anything about a bad System Folder, but they can and will fix a bad disk. This may be all that's required. On the other hand, you may find no trouble with the disk at all, indicating that the problem's with the System Folder instead. In that case, find your original Mac disks, restart your Mac, and insert the one called "Install." Follow the suggestions on the screen and reinstall your System Folder's software.

If after all this you're still getting a blinking question mark, you're up a creek. Get help.

The Keyboard Won't Work

You can ruin a Mac by plugging and unplugging the keyboard cable (and the mouse cable, and just about any other cable) into

Keyboards stop working for two reasons:

1. They're broken, which means a trip to the shop.

2. The cable's loose, which means you're lucky.

Hope for a loose cable.

With the power off, unplug the keyboard cable. Look head-on at the ends. Are the pins bent? That's bad. Are there sharp bends in the cable (possibly from trying to make the cable stretch just a little too far)? That's bad, too. Borrow or buy a keyboard cable and give it a try. That will probably work.

it while the Mac is on. Take a few extra seconds to switch the power off. If you don't, your little "loose keyboard cable" problem may become a big "dead Mac" problem. Seriously.

If a new cable isn't the answer, the problem's in the keyboard. Take it to a shop and have it checked out. Remember to bring your receipt.

The Mouse Won't Work

Mice wear out. Nothing to do about this except get a new one. Naturally you'll want to check the cabling and clean the mouse before you give up on the mouse you have. As with keyboards, be sure the power's off before fooling around with the cables.

Everything's Fine, Then the Screen Goes Black

This is very bad. Probably the Mac's power supply (inside the Mac) is starting to die. Take your Mac to a shop and have it checked out. As usual, check the cables before giving up. Bring your receipt if this is a warranty job.

Sparks Fly Out Of the Floppy Disk Drive and the Whole Thing's Starting to Smoke

This is very *very* bad. Unplug the Mac. Break out the marshmallows and toast them over what used to be your computer. Hope hope hope that it's still under warranty.

And now, the final quiz.

1. What does holding down the Shift key during a restart do? Anything good?

2. Should you buy an extensions manager program?

3. Do you know why they call it "The Chooser?"

4. Have you ordered Safe & Sound?

5. Would you ever reuse a bad floppy disk? Would I?

6. Do you know the difference between "The disk is full" and "There isn't enough memory to run this program?"

7. Do you know the difference between quitting a program and merely closing its windows?

8. How can you speed up your Mac?

9. Should you ever play with the cables while the power's on?

10. How much wood would a woodchuck chuck, if a woodchuck could chuck wood?

Appendix A
Words Your Mother Didn't Use

Actually, these are words *my* mother didn't use, at least not until recently. I feed her a couple of words every couple of months so she can snow the gang at work. So far, it's working.

You can do this, too. Practice using the following words and phrases in sentences so you'll be ready to toss one off when the opportunity arises. Remember, image, image, image.

AppleTalk   Communications scheme built into every Mac and into many printers, enabling these devices to be networked. Example sentence: "That cheapo printer isn't an AppleTalk device."

Bitmapped   Term used to describe certain fonts or graphics where each bit of data is individually mapped onto the screen or paper. Example sentence: "Christian says TrueType or PostScript fonts are best, but I like the look of scaled bitmapped fonts; they're really rad, Man!"

Button   Onscreen graphic that you click on to make selections in dialog boxes and other places. There are OK buttons, Print buttons, and the ever popular Cancel button, to name a few. Example sentence: "Man, she sure knows how to use that Cancel button!"

Byte (rare)   Unit of measure for memory—hard disk, RAM, or ROM. Each character (letter or number or punctuation) takes up one byte of memory. Example sentence: "Don't byte the hand that feeds you."

Cell   The intersection of a column and row in a spreadsheet. Data or formulas are entered into cells. Example sentence: "Wow, did you see what's in cell AA56?"

Chooser   The part of the system software that enables you to choose printers, connections with other Macs, and so on. Example sentence: "Why do they call it Chooser if I only have one printer hooked up to my Mac?"

Consultant   Unemployed Mac aficionado (some exceptions exist). Example sentence: "Christian Boyce is the Macintosh Consultant to the Stars."

Control Panel   Small piece of software that changes the overall Mac environment. Examples include screen savers, clocks, and everything else in the Control Panels folder (look under the **Apple** menu and you'll find it). When you double-click a control panel you get to make choices. You should double-click everything in the Control Panels folder to see what those choices are. Note that many control panels show an icon on the screen when you start up your Mac. Example sentence: "I've got so many control panels, their icons wrap to three rows at startup."

Cursor Keys   The keys on a keyboard that cause the cursor to move in the indicated direction. Example sentence: "I always use the cursor keys, because I am allergic to mice."

Database   A collection of data. Example sentence: "I've got a database of every time Dr. McCoy said 'He's dead, Jim' in Star Trek."

Database Management Program   A program designed to help you manage your databases. Example sentence: "You'd be a fool to buy any other database management program than FileMaker Pro."

Defragment   Rejoining fragmented files and storing them in continuous blocks. Example sentence: "I was going to buy some software that would defragment my hard disk, but Christian said I should buy The Talking Moose instead."

Dialog Box (or **Dialog**, for short)   A conversation between you and your Mac which takes place in a special-purpose onscreen box. The Mac asks you questions; you reply by clicking on buttons, checking off boxes, and typing in words and numbers. Dialog boxes usually have a Cancel button to let you get out of them. Example sentence: "Excel's Page Setup dialog box is as ugly as can be."

Extension   Like Control Panels without controls. Extensions modify the Mac environment, but they don't let you determine how. That is, while control panels let you adjust various settings, extensions don't. Extensions are either on or they're off, simple as that. Example sentence: "What on Earth is the A/ ROSE extension for?"

Field   Each individual item of data in a database. Example sentence: "I've got 45 fields on each of my clients."

Firmware   Software that comes on chips instead of on disks. Firmware is very close to being hardware, but since it theoretically could be changed or updated by replacing the chip, there's a certain non-permanence to it. Example sentence: "I'd like to replace my Mac's firmware, but it looks like Apple's not going to offer an upgrade."

Font   Another word for typeface. There are lots of fonts available in three main types. Do you remember what the types are? (If not, see chapter 7). Example sentence: "I've got 75 fonts installed on my Mac."

Fragmented   The way you feel after trying to figure out how to do a chart in Excel, *or* when electronic files are broken up into segments for storage on a disk. Example sentence: "Many of my files are fragmented, but Christian says not to worry about it."

Gigabyte (or **gig**, with a hard *g*)   One thousand and twenty-four megabytes. This is a BIG bunch of space. Example sentence: "I'm getting a gig drive for my new Quadra."

Handles   The little black boxes that indicate that an object has been selected. They are also used to resize or reshape objects. You see them most often in draw and paint programs and anywhere else where "draw" type tools are used (for example, the layout function in FileMaker Pro). Example sentence: "Man, that rectangle has got some great handles on it!"

Hardware   Pieces of computer machinery. Macs are hardware, monitors are hardware, mice are hardware. Printers are hardware. Keyboards are hardware. Example sentence: "That new PowerBook is a nice piece of hardware."

Icon   The pictures that the Macintosh uses to represent applications, documents, control panels, extensions, hard disks, floppy disks, the trash, and just about everything else. Example sentence: "I just love to work with icons."

Initializing   Preparing a floppy disk for use; also known as erasing. Example sentence: "Whoops, I just initialized that floppy, was there anything important on it?"

Insertion Point   The point on the screen where something will be inserted when letters are typed. In word processors and in text areas of other types of programs, the insertion point is represented with a flashing vertical line. Example sentence: "When I was doing the example in chapter 3, the insertion point was never where Christian said it would be."

Kilobyte (or **K**)   One thousand and twenty-four bytes. Equal to one thousand and twenty-four typed characters, or two-thirds of a single-spaced page. Example sentence: "The scan took 300K of disk space."

Liveware   Computer users. You know, people. Example sentence: "That was a liveware error."

Megabyte (**M** or **meg**)   One thousand and twenty-four kilobytes, or roughly a million bytes. Example sentence: "Microsoft Excel needs five megs of RAM to run."

Object   Something created by a drawing program that has its own characteristics that are distinct from the other objects in a drawing document. Example sentence: "She was the object of his affections."

Optimization   The process of storing files on your hard disk in the most efficient possible fashion. Files used the most but changed the least (such as system software) are stored together, while ever-changing files (such as your bank account) are also kept together "farther out" on the drive. This leads to less fragmentation and faster operation of your drive. Example sentence: "I think these disk optimization programs are really cool."

PhoneNet Connector   Inexpensive adapter that enables you to network AppleTalk devices using modular phone wire. Actually a brand name but used generically to refer to any of several similar devices. Example sentence: "Yup, we've gone totally PhoneNet."

Pixel   An individual dot on the monitor screen. The word is a shortened version of "picture element." How hip! Example sentence: "What was the name of the pixel in Peter Pan?"

Pop-Up Menu   Menu containing a little black triangle which indicates that more choices are available. Pop-up menus can appear in dialog boxes, main menus, or anywhere else in a program. Open one by clicking on the triangle and holding the mouse button down to see what choices you have. Example sentence: "I've got so many pop up-menus, I can't decide what to do."

PowerPC   New generation of Apple computers, which may be just more powerful Macs, but then again they may not be. Since these won't be available until sometime in 1994 you've got a few months to impress the unknowing. Example sentence: "Personally, I'm waiting for the PowerPC."

RAM   Random Access Memory. This is the stuff that your Mac is talking about when it says "There is not enough memory to do what you want." RAM comes on chips about as big as a standard stick of gum. Example sentence: "I need more RAM." By the way, this example sentence is one of the few constants in life. Another is, "I need a bigger hard drive."

RAM is so important that it warrants additional explanation. First, RAM and hard disk space are not the same thing. The typical Mac has much more disk space than RAM, which makes a lot of sense when you know what the two things do. You will soon. Hang in there.

When you copy a program to your hard disk, you've permanently stored it. That program will sit on the hard disk until you delete it (or until the hard disk falls apart). This is sort of like moving that weird shirt Grandma gave you for Christmas into your closet; it's always there, ready for you to use, even if you never do. Thus, hard disks are like closets: places to store lots of things.

When you actually run a program (by double-clicking on it), it's copied from the hard disk into a temporary electronic space called RAM. If the power goes out, the space blanks out, and everything in it is lost (not that this is a disaster, since you've still got the original items on the hard disk). Prime example of RAM gone bad: that blinking "12:00 A.M." on the VCR. The VCR's time is stored in RAM, and when the power goes off—even for an instant—the RAM is totally erased. Start over, do not pass Go.

Running a program is like putting on a shirt. You can only wear so many shirts at a time; after the first couple, you have to take one off before adding another. The only way to avoid the shirt swapping is to get another torso, and the only way to avoid the program swapping is to get some more RAM. Adding RAM itself is painless, except for the "paying for it" part.

ROM   Read-Only Memory. Very different from RAM. RAM is memory to which you can *write* (or send) things and from which you can *read* (or retrieve) things. Read-Only Memory only allows you to (you guessed it) retrieve things from it. Common ROM example: a musical compact disc. A cassette tape (something you can "read" from—that is, play back—and "write" to— that is, record) is an example of RAM. ROM on a Mac refers to a chip that gives a Mac some personality. Example sentence: "The ROM chip is firmware."

SCSI (pronounced "scuzzy")   Small Computer System Interface, a standard cabling and connection scheme for adding hard disks, scanners, CD-ROM drives, tape drives, and other totally cool stuff to your Mac. Example sentence: "Dig it: she's got *six* devices in her SCSI chain."

Software   Computer programs. Microsoft Word is one example of software. So is System 7. So is ClarisWorks. A letter to Dad is not software and neither is a letter to Mom. Example sentence: "The Talking Moose is my favorite Macintosh software."

Spreadsheet   File that looks like a ledger book and consists of columns and rows and is used for math, accounting, and many, many other things. The term is also applied to spreadsheet *programs* that are used to actually generate the spreadsheets. Example sentence: "Christian says that Excel should be referred to as a spreadsheet program, but hey, why not go with the flow and just call it a spreadsheet?"

32-Bit Addressing   Memory location numbering scheme that results in roughly four billion unique addresses. 32-bit addressing allows Macs to access all the RAM their owners can afford. (The previous standard, 24-bit addressing, had an 8-megabyte limit.) Example sentence: "The program doesn't seem to work right with 32-bit addressing turned on."

24-Bit Color   Scheme by which each dot on a monitor is controlled to a very fine degree, resulting in photo-realistic images. Each screen dot, or pixel, is allotted 24 bits of memory. (This has nothing whatsoever to do with 24-bit addressing.) Generally, 24-bit color is necessary only for professional artists. Example sentence: "Her new Mac's got 24-bit color."

Appendix B
Nearly Universal Shortcuts that Almost Always Work

This is such important stuff that I'd put it in front if I were in charge.

Let me tell you how it was.

In the olden days, when Macs were first invented, many Mac users took an almost militant "I like my mouse" approach and avoided the keyboard as much as possible. (I actually spent a whole day playing with my Mac Plus with the keyboard detached, just to see if I could. I could.) Eventually, some of us realized that there was no shame in using the keyboard to make things happen more quickly and easily (especially if no one was watching), and we began exploring the exciting world of Nearly Universal Shortcuts that Almost Always Work. Here are my favorites, culled from years of experience. Try 'em— the time you save will add up.

Menu Item Shortcuts

Command-S almost always Saves. FileMaker is an exception: it sorts. Some other programs also don't use Command-S, but those that don't probably save automatically (for example, Quicken).

Command-P almost always Prints.

Command-O almost always Opens the selected item or brings up the Open dialog box when inside a program.

Command-Q almost always Quits.

Command-Z, -X, -C, and -V   Undo, Cut, Copy, and Paste. The Macintosh Holy Grail. Any program that doesn't adhere to these conventions won't last long on my Mac.

Command-W   almost always Closes the active window.

Command-N   almost always opens a New file. This works in word processing programs, drawing programs, spreadsheet programs—you name it.

Formatting Shortcuts

Command-Shift-B   makes selected text **bold**. (Alternate method: Command-B.)

Command-Shift-I   makes selected text *italic*. (Alternate method: Command-I.)

Command-Shift-U   makes selected text underlined. (Alternate method: Command-U.)

Command-Shift->   increases the size of selected text to next standard Mac size (9-10-12-14-18-24-36-48-60-72).

Command-Shift-<   decreases the size of selected text to next standard Mac size (72-60-48-36-24-18-14-12-10-9).

Selection Secrets

Double-click   a word to select it.

Triple-click   a paragraph to select it.

Shift-click   to extend a selection. With text, click at the beginning of the stuff you want to select, hold the Shift key down, and click at the end of the stuff. Everything in between is selected. With graphics, click on an object, hold the shift, and click on another object. Both objects will be selected (you can continue selecting as many as you like). With icons, click on an icon, hold the Shift key down, and click on another icon. Both icons (again, as many as you like) will be selected.

Command-A   selects All the data in a file. Combine with the shift-click technique, especially in graphics programs and with icons. (Command-A to select All, then shift-click to deselect the undesirables.)

In graphics programs and in the Finder, **click** where there's nothing and drag a rectangle around some items. They'll all be selected. Combine with the shift-click technique for extra flexibility.

If you hold down **Command** and the **mouse button**, you will select any item you touch with the pointer.

Special Places to Click

Double-click   a title bar to zoom it (doesn't work in the Finder).

Command-click   on a Finder window's title bar to see where it comes from. Drag down to open any folder in the list.

Drag   the black bars near scroll arrows to split the screen.

Click   above and below elevator boxes to scroll a window-full of information at a time.

Finder Stuff

Open a folder, then **type the first letter** of what you're looking for. You'll jump to it. Missed? **Press Tab** to move alphabetically, starting from there. **Shift-Tab** moves you backward.

Option-click on a close box to close all open Finder windows.

Choose **Hide Others** from the **Application** menu to unclutter the Desktop.

Index

You've read the book... now get the FAX!

Get *more* timely tips and power techniques from Christian Boyce... TWICE every month!

Subscribe to FAX ON MACS—a practical, step-by-step, "how-to" of Macintosh information that's much more topical than off-the-shelf Mac publications. FAX ON MACS is a single topic one-sheet teeming with tools and tips on all major Macintosh applications. Christian Boyce, author of *Macs for Morons,* writes FAX ON MACS twice a month and sends it to you via fax machine.

Time is precious.

That's why page for page, FAX ON MACS is the fastest reading, easiest to understand, and downright most valuable source of Macintosh secrets available. Anywhere.

Practical, powerful information.

In about the time for coffee and a donut, Christian Boyce's FAX ON MACS can teach you powerful techniques that you can really use. Today. How to make Word behave. How to use aliases. How to master Excel. How to use a modem. And much more.

Get four issues free!

Subscribe to FAX ON MACS for six months for $19.95 and you'll get two issues free. Order 12 months for $34.95 and you'll get *four* issues free.

Send your name, address and fax number, with your payment, to FAX ON MACS, 400 South Beverly Drive, Suite 214, Beverly Hills, California, 90212.

As soon as we receive your order, we'll fax your subscription confirmation and a special introductory issue of FAX ON MACS.

Don't wait. Keep on learning!

Send for your subscription today.

I want the FAX today!

Please accept my subscription to FAX ON MACS. Send my introductory issue right away.

First Name

Last Name

Number & Street

City

State   Zip

Phone

FAX number! **Very important!**

PLEASE CHECK ONE:

6 months subscription
   @ $19.95 *(2 free issues!)*   ☐
12 months subscription
   @ $34.95 *(4 free issues!)*   ☐
Payment enclosed   ☐
Please bill me later   ☐

Send to: **FAX ON MACS**
      400 S. Beverly Drive, Suite 214
      Beverly Hills, CA 90212

Want more Mac facts?
Christian Boyce has also authored *Your Mac Can Do That!*
Published by Hayden Books. Available everywhere.